SQUADRONS!

No. 38

The Supermarine

Spitfire Mk. II

- The Rhodesian, Dominion & Eagle squadrons -

Phil H. LISTEMANN

ISBN: 979-1096490-60-8

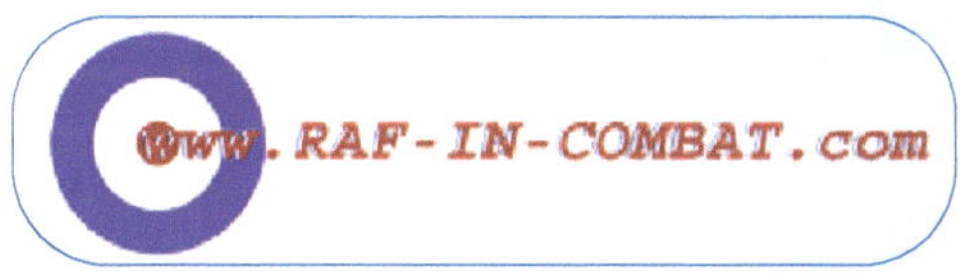

Colour profiles: Gaetan Marie/Bravo Bravo Aviation

GLOSSARY OF TERMS

PERSONEL :

(AUS)/RAF: Australian serving in the RAF
(BEL)/RAF: Belgian serving in the RAF
(CAN)/RAF: Canadian serving in the RAF
(CZ)/RAF: Czechoslovak serving in the RAF
(NFL)/RAF: Newfoundlander serving in the RAF
(NL)/RAF: Dutch serving in the RAF
(NZ)/RAF: New Zealander serving in the RAF
(POL)/RAF: Pole serving in the RAF
(RHO)/RAF: Rhodesian serving in the RAF
(SA)/RAF: South African serving in the RAF
(US)/RAF - RCAF : American serving in the RAF or RCAF

RANKS

G/C : Group Captain
W/C : Wing Commander
S/L : Squadron Leader
F/L : Flight Lieutenant
F/O : Flying Officer
P/O : Pilot Officer
W/O : Warrant Officer
F/Sgt : Flight Sergeant
Sgt : Sergeant
Cpl : Corporal
LAC : Leading Aircraftman

OTHER

ATA: Air Transport Auxiliary
CO : Commander
DFC : Distinguished Flying Cross
DFM : Distinguished Flying Medal
DSO : Distinguished Service Order
Eva. : Evaded
ORB : Operational Record Book
OTU : Operational Training Unit
PoW : Prisoner of War
PAF: Polish Air Force
RAF : Royal Air Force
RAAF : Royal Australian Air Force
RCAF : Royal Canadian Air Force
RNZAF : Royal New Zealand Air Force
SAAF : South African Air Force
s/d: Shot down
Sqn : Squadron
† : Killed

CODENAMES - OFFENSIVE OPERATIONS - FIGHTER COMMAND

CIRCUS:
Bombers heavily escorted by fighters, the purpose being to bring enemy fighters into combat.

RAMROD:
Bombers escorted by fighters, the primary aim being to destroy a target.

RANGER:
Large formation freelance intrusion over enemy territory with aim of wearing down enemy fighters.

RHUBARB:
Freelance fighter sortie against targets of opportunity.

ROADSTEAD:
Dive bombing and low level attacks on enemy ships at sea or in harbour

RODEO:
A fighter sweep without bombers.

SWEEP:
An offensive flight by fighters designed to draw up and clear the enemy from the sky.

THE SUPERMARINE SPITFIRE MK II

Once production of the Spitfire Mk.I was underway, an improved version was looked at based around the 1175hp Merlin XII. Spitfire K9788, then with the A&AEE, was returned to Rolls-Royce in February 1939 to be fitted with the new engine and made its first flight on 30 June. The Spitfire Mk.II, or Supermarine 329 as its constructor named it, was born. Great hopes were placed in this new version as an order for 1000 aircraft was placed on 12 April 1939, before the mark's first flight, for serials **P7280 – P8799**. This production run was launched at Castle Bromwich in Birmingham, the new Supermarine production line. The first aircraft were delivered in June 1940 and the Spitfire Mk.II included all improvements and refinements added to the Spitfire Mk.I. Deliveries continued up to July 1941. The final 79 aircraft of this production run were in fact delivered as the higher performance Mk.V, a version that had entered service some time earlier.

Thus, including the prototype, only 921 Mk.IIs were built, to which we have to add some Spitfire Mk.I conversions, between 1939 and 1941 (making at least 928 Mk.IIs as it seems some conversions were not recorded). Two variants of the Mk.II were developed: the Mk.IIA equipped with eight machine guns (751 aircraft), and the Mk.IIB equipped with two 20mm cannon and four .303 machine guns (170 aircraft). The latter were delivered more towards the end of the production run of the mark as the RAF had decided to change the standard all machine gun armament for a combination of cannons and machine guns. The Mk.II entered service, in the midst of the Battle of Britain, first with 66 Squadron, and 184 had been taken on charge by the end of that famous period. Progressively, the Spitfire Mk.II became standard equipment across Fighter Command with no less than 56 squadrons known to have been equipped, fully or partially, with the mark. Peak usage was reached during the summer of 1941, but, from the autumn of that year, it began to be withdrawn from first line units in favour of the Mk.V. By the spring of 1942, the Mk.II had been completely replaced. A second life was offered to the survivors and many found their way to Operational Training Units. A handful were converted to Spitfire Mk.Vs and fifty more were converted for Air Sea Rescue work, as the ASR.II, equipped with smoke canisters under the port wing and boxes containing a small dinghy and food.

By 1 February 1945, the RAF had approximately 120 Mk.IIs left, the others having been lost in combat, accidents, ceded to the US

Externally, the Spitfire Mk.II (P7508 here) looked very similar to the Spitfire Mk.I, especially from the left, rendering the distinction between the two marks almost impossible. The new Merlin engine variant compensated for the weight gain the Mk.I had acquired since its introduction into service. From a performance point of view, there was no significant increase in speed compared to the early Spitfire Mk.Is, although the rate of climb and service ceiling increased notably.

Among the high-ranking officers from the Dominions who made claims with the Spitfire Mk.II during 1941 was W/C John A. Kent from Winnipeg, Manitoba, in Canada. He joined the RAF in 1935 and was trained as a fighter pilot. At the outbreak of war, he was serving with the RAE at Farnborough. In May 1940, he was posted to the Photographic Development Unit, but it was not until the summer of 1940 that he returned to a fighter unit, 257 Sqn, after a refresher course. This was for a short time, however, as he was called to assist the newly formed 303 (Polish) Squadron as a flight commander. He made his first claims on 9 September 1940. In mid-October he was posted to 92 Sqn, and assumed command a few days later, where he remained until March 1941, continuing to score, until he was rested.

Kent returned to operations in June as the Northolt Wing leader, where he flew the Spitfire Mk.II, before becoming wing leader of the Kenley Wing, still on Mk.IIs, early in August until mid-October when he was rested again. During this period of time he claimed more than five enemy aircraft destroyed. Therefore, he became one of the very few RAF pilots to achieve ace status on the Spitfire Mk.II alone. He survived the war with a DFC and Bar and continued his career with the RAF until 1956.

Navy (4), or transformed into the Mk.V (fifty aircraft beginning in 1942). As soon as the war was over, the RAF underwent a re-organisation and this led to the rapid disposal of the last remaining Mk.IIs. The Spitfire Mk.II is often overshadowed by the Mk.I, the mark that made the aircraft famous during the Battle of Britain, and by the Spitfire Mk.V, the backbone of Fighter Command in 1942 and 1943. It enjoyed a short period during which it served in front line units, but it is mainly remembered as the mark that started the Fighter Command offensive over Europe in the spring of 1941.

THE RHODESIAN, DOMINION AND EAGLE SQUADRONS

Even though the Spitfire II had a relatively short career, it became the mainstay of Fighter Command Spitfire units in 1941. Many squadrons converted from either Hurricanes or the Spitfire Mk.I. Among them were the Rhodesians. While not a Dominion, Southern Rhodesia was a self-governing colony in southern Africa. Many Southern Rhodesians enlisted (and some South Africans who preferred to join the RAF instead of the SAAF) when war broke out and upon completing their training began to arrive at RAF units in 1941. By that time it had been decided that, as far as possible, Rhodesian nationals would be gathered together across various units. For the fighter pilots, 266 Squadron was chosen in January 1941. The number of Rhodesians posted in during 1941 increased steadily and by the autumn of 1941 266 had officially become 266 (Rhodesia) Squadron RAF when the majority of the personnel were Rhodesians. Then, and until the end of the war, the majority of the pilots who served with 266 were Rhodesians or South Africans. The Dominions also saw many of their nationals become operational in 1941. Under Article XV of the Empire Air Training Scheme (EATS), Dominion personnel had to be gathered together in specific units, under RAF control, once trained. The 400-499 squadron numerical range was used for these newly formed units. As far as the Spitfire II was concerned, the type equipped two Australian squadrons (452 and 457), six Canadian units (401, 403, 411, 412, 416 and 417) and New Zealand's 485 Squadron. The RAF could also count on three squadrons manned by American volunteers, the famous 'Eagle' squadrons, with Nos. 71, 121 and 133 initially formed and operational on Hurricanes.

September 1940 October 1940 & March 1941 September 1941

Victories - confirmed or probable claims: 19.66

First operational sortie:
07.09.40
Last operational sortie:
26.09.41

Number of sorties: *ca.* 1,285

Total aircraft written-off: 7

Aircraft lost on operations: 7
Aircraft lost in accidents: -

Squadron code letters:
UO

COMMANDING OFFICERS

S/L Desmond G.H. SPENCER	RAF No. 34114	RAF	...	10.09.40
S/L Patrick G. JAMESON	RAF No. 37813	(NZ)/RAF	10.09.40	09.06.41
S/L Tristam B. de la P. BERESFORD	RAF No. 33156	RAF	09.06.41	...

SQUADRON USAGE

After a short existence at the end of the Great War, this unit was reformed in December 1939 and was intended to be a Blenheim squadron. None were received and, after training with Battles, it began to receive Spitfires in January 1940. The squadron was heavily engaged for the first time over Dunkirk on 2 June 1940 and participated in the Battle of Britain from Wittering. In August 1940, 266 was commanded by S/L D.G.H. Spencer. The arrival of the Spitfire Mk.II was announced on 4 September following information received from HQ Fighter Command. The next day five new Spitfires were delivered by ferry pilots and were followed by thirteen more on the 6th. The squadron was now fully equipped with the new mark (P7285, P7287, P7288, P7289, P7294, P7295, P7296, P7297, P7309, P7310, P7311, P7313, P7324, P7325, P7327, P7350 and P7365). The first operational sorties were flown on the 7th when three pilots were ordered to patrol Yarmouth at 25,000 feet. Only two of them were flying a Mk.II (P/O W.S. Williams, New Zealander in P7285 and P/O R.J.B. Roach in P7309). They were vectored towards enemy aircraft first sighted at 09.00 (the section was airborne at 08.40) west of Norwich at 30,000 feet. The order to attack was given, but due to sun dazzle, the enemy aircraft was twice lost to sight. It was then rediscovered flying at 23,000 feet about 20 miles northwest of Walcheren Island. The chase continued eastwards towards the island. Then the section made a surprise attack. The German bomber took no evasive action, but the German gunners opened fire without result. The Dornier, a Do215, was hit sev-

Squadron Leader P.G. Jameson, a New Zealander, enlisted in the RAF before the war and was already a flight commander with 46 Sqn when the conflict began. He participated in the disastrous Norwegian campaign and was among the very few to survive the sinking of HMS *Glorious* on 8 June 1940. Recovering, he returned to operations to command 266 Sqn in September 1940. He left in June 1941 to become the Wittering Wing leader and continued to take operational positions at Wing level until the end of the war. He was awarded a DSO, DFC and Bar. He continued to serve in the RAF after the war and retired as an Air Commodore in August 1960.

eral times before black smoke poured from the right engine and the bomber went into a vertical dive and crashed into the centre of the island in flames. In the afternoon, a patrol was carried out, but no contact with the enemy was made. The next day, the 8th, another patrol was flown (led by the CO). However, S/L Spencer didn't have time to enjoy his new mount as he was posted out on the 10th to command 257 Squadron (ultimately, he didn't assume this role). He was replaced by S/L P.G. Jameson, a New Zealander serving in the RAF. The next day, six Spitfires went to Duxford for operational duties and in the middle of the morning they were ordered to patrol London as part of a Wing formation. Shortly after leaving the ground a formation of thirty Dorniers was sighted at 22,000 feet over Dartford and Gravesend, followed by a formation of about thirty He-111s with a dozen Bf109s flying as escort above. Within 25 minutes, three bombers were claimed as probably destroyed (Pilot Officers W.S. Williams and R.B.J. Roach, and F/L S.H. Bazley) and five more claimed as damaged (P/O Williams, Sgt R.G.V. Barraclough, and three by P/O H.M.T. Heron). This time the combat was not one-sided as the German gunners hit P/O Roach and he was obliged to bale out. He spent the night at North Weald before returning to the squadron the next day. Patrols on the 15th, 22nd, 24th, 27th, 28th, 29th and 30th were frustrating as none provided the opportunity to engage the enemy. No major changes occurred during the first fortnight of October, but Sgt S.A. Godwin, piloting P7296, made a forced landing with the undercarriage retracted in bad weather at Little Bytham on the 4th. The Spitfire was badly damaged, but it returned to service. The squadron was tasked with patrols, sixty for October, but no engagements took place. However, on the 15th, the CO shot down a barrage balloon that had come loose. This was the last action for 266 while flying the Spitfire II during the Battle of Britain after 139 sorties logged. Indeed, the next day, the squadron was ordered to exchange its Spitfire IIs for 603 Squadron's Mk.Is (603 was based at Hornchurch closer to the main action). The swap was made within 24 hours. The squadron then soldiered on with the older Spitfires until March 1941.

Still based at Wittering, 266 was informed on 7 March it would be re-equipped with Spitfire Mk.IIs again. The first two were delivered by ferry pilots four days later (P7900/W and P7901/U). The re-equipment continued with the delivery of six on the 23rd, one on the 25th, and four on the 26th. The last day of March saw two more arrive. In the meantime, 266 began to fly operations with the first two new aircraft when a patrol was carried out on the 14th. The squadron, however, continued to mainly fly the Mk.I during March. With the delivery of a Mk.II on 3 April, 266 was now fully equipped with the new aircraft, but ops continued with just raid investigations and patrols. Some night patrols were also carried out and, on the night of 9/10 April, S/L Jamieson saw an enemy aircraft flying at 18,000 feet. It was already trailing smoke from each engine and other fighters were nearby. He had turned to give chase and join in when he saw a He111 at about 17,000 feet. He made a stern attack from 150 yards. Four streams of return fire, one of them green (probably from the top turret) was the bomber's reply. Jameson fired two short bursts, but he was dazzled by bullet strikes on the Heinkel so he broke away. He carried out another stern attack and his windscreen was soon obscured by oil from the He111. Great burning pieces fell away from the bomber which dived through the clouds. It was claimed as destroyed. The next night it was the turn to F/L D.L. Armitage to score in claiming a He111 probably destroyed by night near Birmingham. So far the squadron had been tasked with carrying out patrols, but, on 15 April, it flew a Wing sweep (with 65 and 402 Squadrons) between Dungeness and Boulogne, the wing leader, W/C W.E. Coope, flying with 266. When at 20,000 feet they were surprised by Bf109s and Coope's aircraft (P7901) was hit by cannon shells, one of them going through his parachute. He managed to evade and made a crash landing at Manston. He was uninjured and the Spitfire was later repaired. Two other Spitfires were damaged, one of which, P8014, made a crash landing at Hawkinge (P8014 – Sgt Whewell), and no claims were made. On the 17th, the squadron participated in an uneventful defensive sweep. The same day, Sgt C.J.L. Whiteford arrived from 58 OTU. He was the first Rhodesian pilot to be posted in. More would follow. Two days later, in the morning, the squadron was asked to carry out a sweep with 19 Squadron from Duxford to Oxfordness, Margate, Southend, and back to Duxford. No enemy aircraft were seen. In the afternoon another Wing sweep was flown without result. On the 27th, the first two Rhubarb sorties were performed by the CO, with P/O Thomas as wingman, and W/C Coope and P/O W.H. Holland. In both cases, not much was reported on return. The following day, 266 made a Wing patrol with 19 Squadron over the Thames estuary, but nothing was seen. That was the last major action for the month that saw 266 complete more than 250 sorties.

In May, more Rhodesian pilots arrived: Pilot Officers A.J.F. Allen-White and H.L. Parry (from Northern Rhodesia) on the 2nd, Sgt G.L.W. Matthews on the 7th, P/O G.A.F. Buchanan on the 12th, F/O C.L. Green on the 13th, and Sgt D.D. Devenish on the 17th (the latter and Allen-White were actually a South Africans serving with the Rhodesians). Regarding operational activity, excluding a few Rhubarbs, operations consisted of patrols and raid investigations. Operational activity included night patrols, as the German bombers, by spring 1941, were operating at night. Five pilots, including the CO, were airborne just before midnight on the night of 8/9 May and were followed by four more soon after. Patrolling over Derby, S/L P.G. Jameson orbited for about ten minutes when he saw many incendiaries dropping near Nottingham. He was headed to Nottingham when he saw a He111 flying below him on the right beam at about 10,000 feet and on the opposite course travelling west. He did a steep diving turn to the right and attacked the Heinkel from astern and slightly below with a two second burst from about 100 yards. Jameson was blinded by the bullets striking the aircraft and broke away. The He111 climbed steeply, turned almost on its back, stalled and dived vertically without returning fire and apparently out of control. It then disappeared from view against the dark ground and although Jameson dived after it, he was unable to pick it up again. The Heinkel was claimed as probably destroyed. Pilot Officer A.H. Humphrey, meanwhile, claimed

Workers from Castle Browmwich inspect the first Spitfire built at this factory which was operational with 266 as OU-D in September 1940. This Spitfire was usually flown by one of the flight commanders, F/L D.L. Armitage, for the short time 266 used the Mk II during the Battle of Britain.

Charles Green was one of the first Rhodesian pilots to join 266 Sqn in 1941. From Southern Rhodesia, he enlisted in the peacetime RAF and was flying Coastal Command Ansons with 500 Sqn when war broke out. In early 1941 he was posted to 235 Sqn to fly Blenheim fighters until June 1941 when he was posted to 266 Sqn. By September he was one of the flight commanders before becoming the OC in October. He remained at the head of the squadron until July 1943 and oversaw the transition to the Hawker Typhoon in March 1942. He returned to operations, after a rest, in January 1944 at the head of 121 Wing. He retained this position until August when he became OC of 124 Wing. However, despite being a Group Captain, and therefore not allowed to fly on operations, on 26 December 1944, while conducting a ground attack west of St. Vith, during the Battle of Bulge, his Typhoon was hit by flak and he baled out to spend the rest of war as a PoW. He was awarded a DSO and Bar and a DFC.

one He111 as destroyed. He managed to open fire from 150 yards with immediate results as the left engine caught fire. The Heinkel swung to the left as the top gunner returned fire inaccurately. Humphrey continued firing until the gunner was silenced and the right engine glowing and emitting a long stream of smoke. The He111 dived steeply out of control. Two nights later, the same pilots scored again at night, Jameson claiming another He111 (this time destroyed over the Romford area), while Humphrey destroyed two He111s off the Dutch coast. On 15 May, 266 returned to the day fighter game and participated in an uneventful Wing sweep with 19 Squadron from Duxford. Another was flown on the 21st with nothing to report as well. The rest of the month was made up of uneventful patrols and this pattern continued into the first sorties of June. On 4 June, twelve Spitfires of 266 joined 19 Squadron over Duxford for another Wing sweep at 22,000 feet from Dungeness to North Foreland, W/C W.E. Coope flying with 266. In the course of the patrol two small boats were seen about ten miles south east of Dover when Coope's Spitfire was seen to break away, throttled back. The aircraft turned onto its back and spun down and then dived into the sea. No parachute was observed. It was presumed Coope had lost consciousness due to oxygen failure. Without this loss, the op would otherwise have been uneventful. Coope's loss had an immediate impact on the squadron as S/L Jameson was promoted to wing leader of the Wittering Wing. He was replaced by S/L T.B. de la P. Beresford. Later in the month another change took place with the promotion of F/L D.L. Armitage to OC of 129 Squadron, 266 losing a good flight commander in the process. He was replaced by a Rhodesian, F/O C.L. Green. The days that followed were rather quiet, the weather being partially responsible. The new CO flew his first operation with the squadron on the 17th, W/C Jameson flying with his old unit. It was a Wing patrol during which nothing happened. Jameson flew with 266 again for the next major operation on the 21st, another Wing patrol off Dunkirk and cover for bombers returning from raids over the continent. No enemy was sighted, but P/O R.G.V. Barraclough was obliged to make a forced landing in a field due to petrol shortage, fortunately without major consequences to aircraft or pilot. In the afternoon, another Wing patrol was flown, the CO leading, but it was uneventful once again. So far the Luftwaffe had been absent from the sky whenever 266 Squadron was over Europe. Things changed on 23 June. That day, the squadron participated in another Wing sweep with W/C Jameson again flying with 266. The task was to cover bombers leaving France after a raid. The other squadrons were 19 and the New Zealanders of 485. The Luftwaffe was encountered off the coast and numerous attacks were experienced 6 miles inland of Boulogne. The first to make a claim was Jameson who added a Bf109 destroyed to his score. He got it at 20,500 feet by firing a single short burst. He was soon followed by P/O S. Cook who fired a three second burst from slight deflection and immediately saw the Bf109 turn on its back and dive. Cook

Part of A Flight at the end of the summer of 1942. From left to right: F/L C.L. Green, standing, with P/O A.J.F. Allen-White beside him. On his knees is Sgt D.D. Devenish from South Africa (as was Allen-White). Sitting on the wing are Sergeants E.S Dick-Sherwood, J. Plagis (a Greek from Southern Rhodesia), R.H.L. Dawson, D.C. Leggo and C.E. Lees (another South African). Allen-White lost his life the following January 1942 while serving with the squadron. An accident claimed Lees soon after and Leggo died at Malta in March while serving with 249 Sqn. On 19 August 1942, it was Dawson's turn to be posted missing during the Dieppe raid. Devenish and Plagis later served in the Middle East, Devenish taking command of 260 Sqn and, by the end of the war, the Rhodesian 237.
(www.greeks-in-foreign-cockpits.com)

was unable to see whether the Bf109 crashed so only claimed it as probably destroyed. Returning to the coast, he was met by two other Bf109s and engaged the first one, but broke off when the second came to the rescue. Flight Lieutenant R.J.B. Roach engaged a Bf109 and managed to fire a short burst that damaged its left wing. The Germans held their own. Pilot Officer Cunliffe had his Spitfire badly shook up, but managed to return to base. Another Wing sweep was flown on the 25th, but the op was quiet, and two more were flown on the 27th. During the morning sweep, 266 was flying with 19 and 65 Squadrons when Bf109s were engaged near Saint-Omer. Sergeant R.F. Lewis saw a Bf109 attacking a Spitfire and dived after it. He fired three bursts for a total 660 rounds and saw the Bf109 going down in flames. The Bf109s were more accurate this time, however, and two pilots were posted missing. Pilot Officer W.H. Holland became a PoW and P/O S. Cook, who was last seen with a glycol leak following an engagement with a Bf109, was killed. The sweep carried out in the afternoon was uneventful as was the last sweep of the month on the 30th.

On 3 July, the squadron left West Malling with 257 and 401 (RCAF) Squadrons for an offensive sweep, 266 flying as the third and top squadron. About fifty enemy aircraft were encountered over Hazebrouck and combat was engaged. Squadron Leader T.B. de la P. Beresford saw Bf109s slightly to the left and flying towards to the squadron. He noted the right hand one was lagging and got on its tail. He fired a five second burst from 200 yards, closing to 100 yards, and saw it smoking as it dived vertically. His wingman, Sgt D.D. Devenish, saw the 109 hit the ground and the claim was made for a confirmed victory. It wasn't over for the CO, however, who almost immediately saw three more Bf109s flying 2000 feet above and turning sharply to the left. The first two peeled off and attacked the section behind him while the third Bf109 continued to climb and turn until it stalled. Beresford was able to close to about 70 yards during his climb and managed to fire a three second burst. The Bf109 dropped away from its stall and spun towards the ground. As no further action could be undertaken, it could only be claimed as damaged. The CO had fired 1300 rounds during the two actions. He was not the only one to score. Pilot Officer R.G.V. Barraclough claimed one Bf109 as destroyed, while Sgt C.J.L. Whiteford claimed one probably destroyed. Whiteford also claimed a Bf109 as damaged, as did Sergeants A.J.F. Allen-White and J.E. van Schaick (his claim was later upgraded to probably destroyed). On the debit side, Sgt G.L.W. Matthews was posted missing, believed killed, and Sgt R.J. Thoburn, was also posted missing, but was later reported as a PoW. Over the next few days, 266 was tasked to carry out patrols and did not return to the continent until the 11th. Wing Commander Jameson flew with 266 as the squadron joined 65 Squadron and the Australians of 452. The operation was uneventful and a return to more defensive tasks filled the following days. On 19 July, flying in pairs from midday, 266 patrolled over a destroyer carrying out diving operations about 15 miles north of Sheringham. The same day, Sergeants G. Elcombe and I.M. Munro, both Rhodesians, and J. Plagis, a Greek who had

Of Greek parents who emigrated to Southern Rhodesia, John Plagis joined the SRAF when war broke out. Once his training was complete he was sent to the UK where he served initially with 65 Sqn before joining 266 in July 1941. In January 1942 he volunteered to serve overseas and was sent to Malta, being posted to 249 Sqn on arrival after delivering a Spitfire to the island. He distinguished himself in the defence of the island and left Malta in July 1942 with a DFC and Bar, as a flight commander with 185 Sqn, and as one of the most successful fighter pilots of this period.
He returned to the UK and led 126 Sqn for a second tour of operations, later becoming wing leader of the Bentwaters Wing on Mustang IIIs, and was made a Companion of the DSO. After a brief spell with the RAF he returned to Southern Rhodesia and eventually became a Rhodesian citizen.

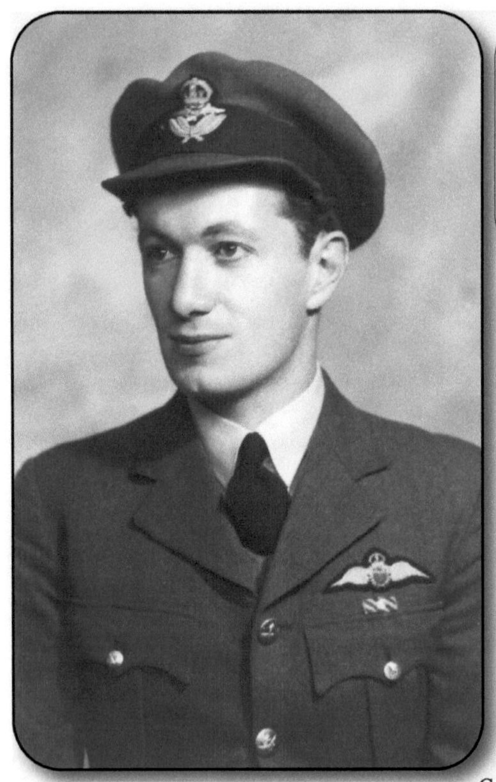

been living in Southern Rhodesia, arrived at the squadron. Two days later, 266 returned over the continent as part of a Wing sweep. While enemy aircraft were seen, no combats ensued. Another sweep followed on the 23rd, 266 flying with 601 and 401 (RCAF) Squadrons. This time the Bf109s were met and while F/L C.L. Green and Sgt D. Leggo (both Rhodesians) managed to engage, initially at long range, then closer, no claims were made. Pilot Officer A.C. Johnston became separated from the squadron and was attacked by four Bf109s. He was lucky not to be hit and in turn fired at three of his attackers, but without results. On the 25th, the squadron saw a change of pace with a Rhubarb carried out by W/C P.G. Jameson and P/O A.J.F. Allen-White (Rhodesian). That was the last sortie of interest for the month. In August, more Rhodesian pilots continued to arrive, initially Sergeants A. Spence-Ross, V.L. Carine, W.R. Smithyman, R.A. Hardy and C.D. Browne early in the month, with Pilot Officers J.D. Wright and N.N. Allen following later. It was a short stay for some. Sergeant C.D. Browne lost his life on 11 August at Hawarden while at 57 OTU for additional training, while Sgt Elcombe was posted to 19 Squadron, Spence-Ross to 129 and P/O G.A.F. Buchanan and Sgt C.J.L. Whiteford went to 41. On the 20th, the squadron was officially titled 'Rhodesia'. Finally, Sgt V.C. Carine was killed on the 31st while taking off to investigate a raid. He struck the maintenance hangar with his left wing. The Spitfire crashed and caught fire, leaving no chance for the pilot. The squadron was kept busy that month flying mainly patrols or scrambles with only a few offensive ops carried out – a Rhubarb on the 7th with four aircraft, that included W/C Jameson and the CO, to the Dutch coast, and another by two Spitfires two days later. The squadron had to wait until the 12th to operate at full strength when it took part in a Wing sweep, with 65 and 19 Squadrons, escorting Blenheims. As usual W/C Jameson was flying with 266. The Bf109s were engaged south of Haamstede and while several pilots fired their guns, only the

Four NCOs from Southern Rhodesia From left to right: C.E. Lees, J. Plagis, V.C. Carine and D. Leggo. Victor Carine was lost soon after on 31 August 1941. Behind is the Spitfire II usually flown by John Plagis, P8092/UO-D.
(www.greeks-in-foreign-cockpits.com)

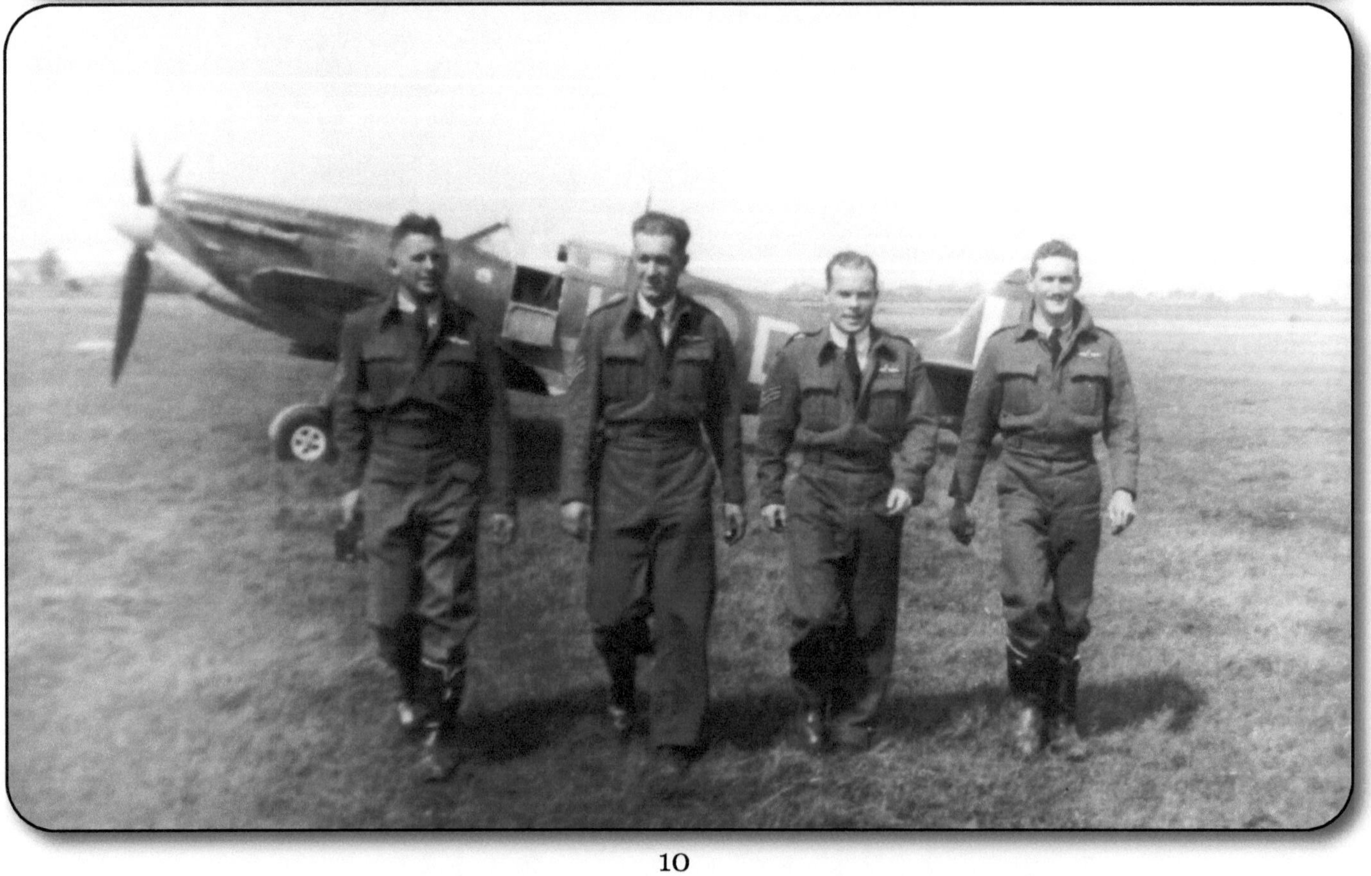

Douglas Leggo with one of the recently arrived cannon-armed Spitfire IIBs, P8505/OU-H. *(A. Thomas)*

wing leader was able to file a claim for a damaged Bf109, proving the combat was rather balanced. If we ignore a few holes, the Rhodesians returned unscathed. Two days later, while on a dusk patrol, a Do17 was intercepted, but here, too, the combat ended in anti-climax as the Dornier escaped into the approaching darkness and its return fire was inaccurate. The squadron had better luck a couple of days later on 19 August during another dusk patrol when a He111 was seen and intercepted. Flight Lieutenant McMullen and Sgt Munro turned and attacked from the left quarters at 150 yards range. Thereafter, twelve attacks from all angles were made almost alternatively by each pilot and 5000 rounds of ammunition were fired. Considerable, though inaccurate, return fire was experienced and it stopped when the Heinkel suddenly dropped its nose and disappeared into the sea, leaving no survivors or wreckage. Two days later F/L McMullen encountered another He111 at dusk, but the combat proved inconclusive and no claim was made, the He111 escaping into the fading light. By the end of the month, only one more major operation a squadron sweep on the 28th, had been completed. The final days of the month were quiet, leaving 266 with almost 200 sorties flown for August.

In September, more Rhodesians arrived, starting with Sgt R.G.G. Gain on the first day of the month, and followed by Sgt J.H. Deall on the 2nd. Later in the month, Sergeants Welby, Howard, Miller and MacNamara, as well as P/O G.R.M. Bell, were posted in. September was the month when the first Spitfire IIB cannon-equipped fighters were taken on charge, the first two arriving on the 3rd (P8643 and P8509). The pilots knew these new arrivals were temporary as they had been forewarned 266 was to fully re-equip with Spitfire Vs. Nevertheless, perhaps to get the pilots and groundcrew used to the new armament, more Spitfire IIBs arrived during the month (P8464, P8503, P8505/H, P8527, P8644, P8648, P8665 and P8666). Operational activity mostly consisted of patrols early in the month with only one Rhubarb by four Spitfires flown in the first ten days. A 1000 ton ship was strafed south west of Zierikzee. This was followed by another Rhubarb on the morning of the 11th and a Wing sweep in the afternoon with 56 and 601 Squadrons. All of the sorties were uneventful. On 12 September F/L D.A.P. McMullen led a Rhubarb in the early afternoon, but, after attacking a sailing vessel, P/O H.L. Parry became separated and was engaged by six Bf109s. They probably thought a lone Spitfire was easy prey, but Parry managed to escape into cloud. On emerging, he saw two Bf109s in front of him and fired instinctively, sending one of them into the sea. A dusk patrol was led by F/L McMullen in the evening. When north of Smiths Knoll, McMullen saw a He111 at 2000 feet flying a reciprocal course. He turned on to its tail. He closed in and, from a range of 200 yards, fired a six second burst, closing to 150 yards. While McMullen saw the left engine on fire, the Heinkel disappeared in to cloud so it could only be claimed as a probable. He then saw another He111 attacking a convoy and engaged, but no results were seen. Three days later, 266 scored again during a Rhubarb flown by W/C P.G. Jameson and Sgt E.C. Dicks-Sherwood. About 40 miles from the Dutch coast, Sherwood saw four Bf110s astern. The two pilots turned and met the enemy head on. Fire was exchanged, but with no result. Then Jameson got on the tail of one and, with a two second burst, sent it in to the sea, while Dick-Sherwood, attacking a second, managed to fire a burst and saw a large flash in the cockpit. On return he filed a claim for a damaged Bf110. September 17 was a busy day with convoy patrols and two uneventful sweeps, but that was also the day when the squadron introduced the Spitfire V into action. While only one Mk.V was deployed, it was the beginning of the end for the Spitfire II. More Spitfire Vs increasingly took part in operations as the month progressed (including a couple of offensive sweeps with the Wing). The Spitfire IIs were seeing very little use and a claim on the 26th was made by a Mk.V. By the end of the month, 266 was fully equipped with the new aircraft, the last Spitfire IIs leaving the squadron in early October to be allocated to other units.

Claims - 266 Squadron (Confirmed and Probable)

Date	Pilot	SN	Origin	Type	Serial	Code	Nb	Cat.
07.09.40	P/O Wycliff S. **WILLIAMS**	RAF No. 42173	(NZ)/RAF	Do215	**P7285**		0.33	C
	P/O Robert J.B. **ROACH**	RAF No. 42263	RAF		**P7309**		0.33	C
	Shared with P/O R.M. Trousdale flying a Spitfire Mk I							
11.09.40	F/L Sydney H. **BAZLEY**	AAF No. 90359	RAF	Do215	**P7288**		1.0	P
	P/O Robert J.B. **ROACH**	RAF No. 42263	RAF	He111	**P7313**	UO-W	1.0	P
	P/O Wycliff S. **WILLIAMS**	RAF No. 42173	(NZ)/RAF	He111	**P7285**		1.0	P
09.04.41	S/L Patrick G. **JAMESON**	RAF No. 37813	(NZ)/RAF	He111*	**P7892**	UO-K	1.0	C
10.04.41	F/L Dennis L. **ARMITAGE**	RAF No. 76573	RAF	He111*	**P8010**	UO-A	1.0	P
09.05.41	S/L Patrick G. **JAMESON**	RAF No. 37813	(NZ)/RAF	He111*	**P8187**	UO-B	1.0	P
	P/O Andrew H. **HUMPHREY**	RRAF No. 33543	RAF	He111*	**P8170**	UO-M	1.0	C
11.05.41	S/L Patrick G. **JAMESON**	RAF No. 37813	(NZ)/RAF	He111*	**P7892**	UO-K	1.0	C
	P/O Andrew H. **HUMPHREY**	RAF No. 33543	RAF	He111*	**P8170**	UO-M	2.0	C
23.06.41	W/C Patrick G. **JAMESON**	RAF No. 37813	(NZ)/RAF	Bf109	**P8422**		1.0	C
	P/O Stanley **COOK**	RAF No. 66488	RAF	Bf109	**P8187**	UO-B	1.0	P
27.06.41	Sgt Raymond F. **LEWIS**	RAF No. 754684	RAF	Bf109	**P8187**	UO-B	1.0	C
03.07.41	S/L Tristam B. de la Poer **BERESFORD**	RAF No. 33156	RAF	Bf109	**P8515**	UO-E	1.0	C
	P/O Ronald G.V. **BARRACLOUGH**	RAF No. 66487	RAF	Bf109	**P8597**		1.0	C
	Sgt Cyril J.L. **WHITEFORD**	RAF No. 777750	(SR)/RAF	Bf109	**P8422**		1.0	P
	Sgt John E. **VAN SCHAICK**	RAF No. 758018	RAF	Bf109	**P8167**	UO-N	1.0	P
19.08.41	F/L Desmond A.P. **McMULLEN**	RAF No. 40002	RAF	He111	**P7850**		0.5	C
	Sgt Ian M. **MUNRO**	RAF No. 778349	(SR)/RAF		**P8422**		0.5	C
12.09.41	P/O Hugh L. **PARRY** [1]	RAF No. 89399	RAF	Bf109	**P8597**		1.0	C

Total: 19.66

* by night

[1] From Northern Rhodesia

Summary of the aircraft lost on Operations - 266 Squadron

Date	Pilot	S/N	Origin	Serial	Code	Fate
11.09.40	P/O Robert J.B. **ROACH**	RAF No. 42263	RAF	**P7313**	UO-W	-
04.06.41	W/C William E. **COOPE**	RAF No. 05201	RAF	**P8034**		†
27.06.41	P/O Stanley **COOK**	RAF No. 66488	RAF	**P8188**		†
	P/O William H. **HOLLAND**	RAF No. 86664	RAF	**P8185**		**PoW**
03.07.41	Sgt Gordon W.L. **MATTHEWS**	RAF No. 777634	(SR)/RAF	**P8566**		†
	Sgt Reginald J. **THOBURN**	RAF No. 754132	RAF	**P8173**		**PoW**
31.08.41	Sgt Victor L. **CARINE**	RAF No. 778273	(SR)/RAF	**P8471**		†

Total: 7

An Australian serving in the RAF, S/L R.W. Bungey flew as a Fairey Battle pilot with 226 Sqn in France and volunteered to serve in Fighter Command during the Battle of Britain. He was then posted to 145 Sqn where he claimed two shared confirmed victories and was shot down once. After commanding 452 Sqn during its most successful period, he left with another confirmed victory and a DFC. Bungey did not fly on operations again, holding various staff positions before transferring to the RAAF in January for repatriation to Australia. He tragically died there on 10.06.43.

No. 452 (RAAF) Squadron (code UD)

This unit was the first Australian squadron formed in Britain during the Second World War. It was formed at Kirton in Lindsey on 8 April 1941 under the command of S/L Roy Dutton, a very experienced British pilot. The flight commanders were also experienced RAF pilots, with F/L B.E.F. Finucane, an Irishman, as A Flight CO, and F/L A.G. Douglas at the head of B Flight. The squadron worked up on the Spitfire Mk.I before receiving the first Spitfire Mk.IIs, in May, while still awaiting the arrival of more pilots. The first six Spitfire Mk.IIs were taken on charge on 18 May. The squadron was declared partially operational on 22 May and the first patrol was carried out, while at readiness, that day. This first patrol was flown by Australian Sergeants K.L. Milne and A.C. Roberts. By the end of the month more patrols or convoy escorts had been flown, but the work rate was low with only ten sorties recorded by 31 May. At that time 452 had the following aircraft on charge: P7524, P7567, P7590, P7657, P7682, P7786/C, P7789, P7853/Y, P7858, P8038, P8040, P8041, P8073, P8081, P8085, P8099, P8130 and P8361. In June operational activity increased, helped by the fact that 452 was declared fully operational on the 2nd. Besides the usual patrols and convoy protection, some interceptions were made. On 10 June F/L Finucane and A.G. Sgt Costello (RAAF) scrambled and sighted a Ju88, but lost it in cloud. The next day, P/O R.E. Thorold-Smith (RAAF) crashed on take off from Sutton Bridge for an air-firing exercise. This was the only accidental loss during the unit's Spitfire Mk.II era. On 15 June, F/L R.W. Bungey, an Australian serving in the RAF, and a veteran of the Battles of France and Britain, assumed command. Another enemy aircraft was sighted on 21 June, but no interception completed. June ended with 127 sorties carried out, but with little to report.

July started poorly. While the intensity of the operational activity was maintained, Sgt A.G. Costello became the first member of 452 Squadron to lose his life (and in a most unexpected way). Returning from a night training flight in the middle of the night of 4/5 July, he was caught by surprise by a German intruder and shot down while preparing to land at North Coates aerodrome. He did not survive the crash. The pilots had to wait about a week to have their revenge. After many days of convoy patrols or uneventful scrambles, twelve aircraft were sent on a fighter sweep led by the CO over the continent. They were part of a Wing formation comprising 65 and 266 Squadrons. The Wing crossed the French coast around Dunkirk, 266 leading at 17,000 feet while 452 was flying at 18,000 feet and 65 at 19,000. Soon after, the Wing split up and, almost immediately, Bf109s were sighted. It was not long before they attacked and selected the section led by F/L Finucane. Combat was engaged and Finucane achieved an advantage over one of the attackers and claimed it as destroyed, the German pilot being seen to bale out by Finucane and Sgt Hanigan. The Germans were successful too, however, as Sgt A.C. Roberts was hit and obliged to evacuate his aircraft in mid-air. He was not taken prisoner, though. Indeed, he walked to Calais and the French Resistance helped him to evade via Spain and Gibraltar. Roberts returned to the UK three months later and was back with the squadron in November before being sent to the Far East several months later. The following days were quiet, but the move to Kenley on the 22nd was a major change and, on the following day, 452 participated in two uneventful fighter sweeps. The next two on the 23rd were as well even though Bf109s were seen nearby and some pilots fired their guns. The 24th was a different matter. Returning at 14,000 feet from a morning offensive sweep over Cherbourg, two Bf109s were suddenly seen diving steeply onto the right section of 452. Pilot Officer A.H. Humphrey attacked the second aircraft from the beam, rounding into the quarter, and fired a one second burst from 50 yards. The Bf109 pulled out violently and half of its tail fell off. It was seen diving steeply and turning slowly to the right before hitting the water. The pressure on 452 was reduced until the end of the month, a month that ended with a bomber escort on the 31st without incident. This op allowed the squadron to achieve more than 200 sorties for July. Regarding operations, August started on the 3rd with a *Rhubarb*, carried out by the CO and Sgt C.G.B. Chapman (RAAF), and F/L B.E.F. Finucane and Sgt R.G. Gazzard (RAAF), that took place in the middle of the afternoon during which Finucane fired at a motor vessel, silencing one gun. In the evening, 452 performed a sweep. After crossing the coast, they were warned Bf109s were approaching from the rear and right of the formation. They were soon spotted flying in line astern. They half rolled behind 452 and made an

attack from the squadron's right. Flight Lieutenant Finucane broke away with his section to attack the Bf109s and was soon in a position where he could fire a burst that missed the Bf109 he was after. He followed the Bf109 into a thin layer of cloud and, as he was turning away, he saw the German pilot's wingman going down in flames thanks to P/O W.D. Eccleton's gunfire. Finucane managed to stay in touch with his quarry by following its condensation trail and, as they broke cloud, found himself about 200 yards from the Bf109. He immediately fired a burst that set the Bf109 on fire. Soon after, Finucane saw eighteen Bf109s patrolling above in a circle, apparently following a leader. Finucane attacked and fired two bursts at one of them. Following hits on the tail, the second burst saw the Bf109 descend vertically, apparently out of control. Finucane lost sight of it, however, and could only claim a probable. All pilots returned to base. While the first Spitfire Mk.Vs had begun to arrive, the next offensive operation was carried out on the 7th with the Wing over Saint-Omer (*Circus* 67). It proved uneventful. The following foray (*Circus* 68 over Gosnay), which took place two days later, would generate a lot of paperwork! Intercepted between Mardyck and Béthune, the combat that ensued led to the destruction of five Bf109s claimed by five pilots: F/L B.E.F. Finucane, and the Australian Pilot Officers D.E. Lewis, R.E. Thorold-Smith and K.W. Truscott, and Sgt K.B. Chisholm (RAAF). This time, however, not all of the pilots made the return journey. Pilot Officer J.H. O'Byrne and Sergeants G.B. Haydon and C.G.B. Chapman, all Australians were taken prisoner, but the wounded Haydon died a couple of days later. The squadron was again present over the continent during the next two days, but no combat was engaged and the ops were carried out without incident. Circus 72 of 14 August was similarly uneventful. The 15th was rainy with no operational flying, but 452 returned to the continent on the evening of the 16th (*Circus* 73) with 602 Squadron and the New Zealanders of 485. The Australians had been flying with a mixed force of Mk.IIs and Mk.Vs for a few days, the latter having been recently introduced to operations. A number of enemy aircraft were sighted on the way to the target, but they did not attack. On the return from the target enemy aircraft (about 10-15) were again sighted, but this time they were seen diving. Finucane shot a Bf109 down in flames with a burst delivered from 75 yards and, almost immediately after, shot down another one by blowing off its tail from 10 yards. He made his claims flying a Mk.II, as did Australian Sgt A.R. Stuart (Finucane had scored while flying a Spitfire V that morning). While other claims were made, they came from pilots flying the new aircraft. On the 18th, 452 participated in two Wing sweeps after midday, in company of 452 (NZ) and 602 Squadrons (the Kenley Wing), during which only a small amount of flak was experienced on the first one. The second sweep, Circus 80, saw the Luftwaffe engaged while the squadron was flying at 16,000 feet. Attacked by four Bf109s, only Finucane managed to be in a good enough position to engage, but no results were observed. The combat ended with no claims or losses on either side. Use of the Spitfire Mk.II was now limited with only a few aircraft participating in each sweep as 452 was now mainly using the Mk.V. Again, a mixed force was used the following day, the 19th. A Wing sweep (*Circus* 81) with 485 and 602 was flown very late in the morning and fierce combat took place over the Gravelines-Gosnay area. The squadron was flying at 20,000 feet and on the left of the formation when it was attacked. Only three pilots, including Finucane and Douglas, the two flight commanders, were flying the older Spitfires. The squadron sustained losses (two Mk.Vs see *SQUADRONS!* 75), but as far as the Mk.IIs were concerned, only Finucane was able to score, returning with a Bf109 confirmed and another probably destroyed. The Mk.II almost disappeared from 452's inventory during the following days, only being used when not enough Mk.Vs were available. That was the case for *Circus* 87 on 26 August when two of the older fighters were flown by Sergeants J.R.H. Elphick and A.R. Stuart, both RAAF. Over Gravelines, the squadron was attacked and Stuart managed to make one of the two claims recorded that day, a Bf109 destroyed. This was the swansong for the Spitfire Mk.II and 452 Squadron as, the next day, its final sorties were recorded, one during a morning sweep, and another escorting a Lysander (Sgt K.B. Chislom flew this op). The final Spitfire IIs left soon after. The squadron had flown just over 450 sorties with the mark.

Like many Spitfire squadrons formed in 1941, Mk.Is were used for working up before Mk.IIs were flown operationally. However, Mk.Vs soon replaced the older models, allowing the squadron to achieve significant results at the end of summer and autumn 1941. The Spitfire Mk.II seen landing is P7786/UD-C and was regularly flown by Sgt Keith Chisholm, a pilot who became an ace while flying with 452 Sqn. He made his first two claims with this aircraft on 09.08.41.

Date	Pilot	SN	Origin	Type	Serial	Code	Nb	Cat.
11.07.41	F/L Brendan E.F. **Finucane**	RAF No. 41276	(IRE)/RAF	Bf109	**P8038**		1.0	C
24.07.41	P/O Andrew H. **Humphrey**	RAF No. 33543	RAF	Bf109	**P7973**		1.0	C
03.08.41	F/L Brendan E.F. **Finucane**	RAF No. 41276	(IRE)/RAF	Bf109	**P8038**		1.0	C
							1.0	P
	P/O William D. **Eccleton**	Aus. 402232	(NZ)/RAAF	Bf109	**P8264**		1.0	C
09.08.41	F/L Brendan E.F. **Finucane**	RAF No. 41276	(IRE)/RAF	Bf109	**P8038**		1.5	C
	Sgt Keith B. **Chisholm**	Aus. 402150	RAAF	Bf109	**P7786**	UD-C	0.5	C
	P/O Donald E. **Lewis**	Aus. 402148	RAAF	Bf109	**P7853**	UD-Y	0.5	C
	Sgt Keith B. **Chisholm**	Aus. 402150	RAAF	Bf109	**P7786**	UD-C	0.5	C
	P/O Keith W. **Truscott**	Aus. 400213	RAAF	Bf109	**P7973**		1.0	C
	F/L Brendan E.F. **Finucane**	RAF No. 41276	(IRE)/RAF	Bf109	**P8038**		0.5	C
	P/O Raymond E. **Thorold-Smith**	Aus. 402144	RAAF	Bf109	**P8381**		0.5	C
16.08.41	F/L Brendan E.F. **Finucane**	RAF No. 41276	(IRE)/RAF	Bf109	**P8170**		2.0	C
	Sgt Archibald R. **Stuart**	Aus. 402141	RAAF	Bf109	**P8518**	RF-J*	1.0	C
19.08.41	F/L Brendan E.F. **Finucane**	RAF No. 41276	(IRE)/RAF	Bf109	**P8170**		1.0	C
							1.0	P
26.08.41	Sgt Archibald R. **Stuart**	Aus. 402141	RAAF	Bf109	**P8148**	UD-F	1.0	C

Total: 16.0

*On loan from 303 (Polish) Sqn

Date	Pilot	S/N	Origin	Serial	Code	Fate
05.07.41	Sgt Andrew G. **Costello**	Aus. 404086	RAAF	**P8085**		†
11.07.41	Sgt Alexander C. **Roberts**	Aus. 402007	RAAF	**P7562**		Eva.
09.08.41	P/O Justin H. **O'Byrne**	Aus. 408022	RAAF	**P7682**		PoW
	Sgt Gerald B. **Haydon**	Aus. 404100	RAAF	**P8361**		†
	Sgt Christopher G.B. **Chapman**	Aus. 404198	RAAF	**P7590**		PoW

Total: 5

Date	Pilot	S/N	Origin	Serial	Code	Fate
11.06.41	P/O Raymond E. **Thorold-Smith**	Aus. 402144	RAAF	**P8130**		-
		Total: 1				

No. 457 (RAAF) Squadron (code BP)

Formed on 16 June 1941, the squadron was initially manned by Australian pilots and RAF groundcrew. It worked up on the Spitfire Mk.I and, on 5 August, became officially operational and was sent to Jurby on the Isle of Man. The squadron was well led with S/L P.M. Brothers as CO, and Flight Lieutenants H.L. North and A.L. Edy as flight commanders. None of this leadership group was Australian. Harold was a New Zealander, and Edy a Canadian, and both were serving with the RAF on Short Service Commissions. There was not much to do operationally. Routine and practice flights occupied the day with just convoy patrols to break up the monotony. Things didn't change with the arrival of the first Spitfire Mk.IIs on 29 September: P7368, P7438, P7445, P7756, P7696, P7776, P7818, P7905, P7917, P8017, P8090, P8175, P8360, P8380 and P8425, followed a few days later by P7280, P7529 and P8041. As the Spitfire Mk.Is were progressively allotted to other units, mostly OTUs, the new aircraft began to succeed them on operations (the first logged on 8 October). By the end of October, 29 sorties had been achieved. By that time, the nature of 457 had changed and it had become an unofficial post-OTU squadron for the benefit of 452 Squadron located in the south and heavily engaged. Therefore, the turnover of pilots was high from late 1941 into early 1942. Many practice flights were flown, some minor mishaps recorded, and operational activity remained low (continuing with patrols and rare scrambles) with about thirty sorties flown in November. It was during the course of a patrol that Sgt R.T. Brewin (RAAF) was posted missing on the 29th. He lost the formation in cloud and it was presumed he had ditched into the sea. His body was later sighted floating face down. A few days later another drama occurred when the B Flight CO, F/L Edy (RCAF), was killed in a flying accident on 5 December. He had taken off for a practice flight. The weather was good, but he crashed fifteen minutes later. It was believed the engine of his aircraft caught fire over Ramsey. He baled out too low for his parachute to open properly. He was replaced by F/L J.A.A. Gibson, a New Zealander serving in the RAF, on the 15th. December was also the month the first Spitfire Mk.Vs began to arrive. The process to re-equip was slow and operational flights carried out on both types continued for a while. On 31 December, Sgt R.N.B. Stevens (RAAF), returning from a practice flight, found his aircraft veering to the right on touching down. It ran off the runway and turned over on its back as it came to a halt. Stevens was slightly injured, and was admitted to hospital, but the aircraft was too badly damaged to repair. No major consequences neither for Stevens, as he would later command 451 Squadron in 1943-1944. In the first weeks of 1942, the Spitfire Mk.IIs continued to disappear from the squadron's inventory and the last were sent away in February 1942. The last of the mark's 98 sorties with 457 Squadron was on 14 February.

An unidentified Spitfire Mk II of 457 Squadron coded BP-N at Jurby at the end of the summer of 1941.

Summary of the aircraft lost on Operations - 457 (RAAF) Squadron

Date	Pilot	S/N	Origin	Serial	Code	Fate
29.11.41	Sgt Raymond T. **Brewin**	Aus. 400458	RAAF	**P7445**		†
31.12.41	Sgt Reginald N.B. **Stevens**	Aus. 404672	RAAF	**P7905**		-

Total: 2

Summary of the aircraft lost by accident - 457 (RAAF) Squadron

Date	Pilot	S/N	Origin	Serial	Code	Fate
05.12.41	F/L Allen L. **Edy**	RAF No. 41566	(CAN)/RAF	**P7502**		†

Total: 1

THE CANADIANS

No. 401 (RCAF) Squadron (code YO)

Having arrived in Britain as 1 Squadron RCAF to participate in the Battle of Britain, this unit was renamed 401 (RCAF) Squadron in March 1941. It was equipped with Hurricanes. The squadron transitioned to the Spitfire II from the second week of September 1941, but this only lasted about three to four weeks. The aircraft known to have been used were P7430/N, P7564, P7610/E, P7893, P7908/Q, P7987/X, P8080, P8169, P8179/P, P8191/S, P8392, P8393, P8396, P8423, P8436, P8652/W and P8702. They were soon replaced by Mk.Vs on which the squadron became operational in October. Most of the Mk.IIs had left by 20 October. However, two, P7430 and P7564, remained on strength until early 1942 to serve as training aircraft and hacks.

No. 403 (RCAF) Squadron (code KH)

This unit was formed on 1 March 1941 and was the first of 35 RCAF squadrons to be formed overseas. It came into being at the same time the RCAF overseas was re-organised, as was the denomination of the squadrons based in UK. Command of 403 was given to S/L B.G. Morris of the RAF. It worked up on Curtiss Tomahawks, but they were soon discarded for Spitfire Mk.Is from May 1941. These were replaced by Mk.IIs in July. At that time the squadron was at Ternhill, south of Liverpool, and had become operational. Far from the front line, 403 was occupied with improving its standard and flying patrols and scrambles. The first five Mk.IIs was taken on hand on 14 July. The switch was made in the following days with the arrival of other Mk.IIs while the older Mk.Is departed. By the 30th, the following Spitfire Mk.IIs were on strength: P7280/N, P7352/R, P7355/V, P7368/J, P7422/O, P7622/M, P7744/E, P7746/K, P7756/U, P7825/C, P7911/B, P7917/W, P8090/H, P8233/L, P8373/T, P8377/P, P8380/F, P8425/D, P8546/A and P8726/G. Sadly, the arrival of the new Spitfires was marked by the death of Sgt L. Girman on 30 July. He lost control while flying in cloud during a practice flight, diving into the ground and catching fire. In the meantime, the squadron had carried out its first operational sorties when F/O D.J. McKenna and Sgt J.B.B. Rainville both RCAF scrambled on the 18th. Two days later, the Spitfire Mk.II had the opportunity to open its account when two aircraft were sent to shoot down a loose balloon.

Things became more serious when, on 4 August, the squadron moved south to Hornchurch to carry out operations over the continent. It was re-equipped with the Spitfire Mk.V for the task. After two weeks of operations at Hornchurch, 403 moved to Debden, but reverted to Mk.IIs. The squadron was now led by a new CO, S/L R.A. Lee-Knight, who replaced S/L B.G. Morris after the latter was shot down and captured on 21 August. The following week 403 did not fly on operations and dedicated its time to training. However, on the 27th, the squadron moved back to Hornchurch to carry out a Circus, a bomber escort to Lille. Over Lille, Bf109s

403 Squadron, August 1941:
Back row: P/O D.A.S. Colvin (RAF), P/O C.P.J. Wood (RAF - †14.04.42), F/L E.C. Cathels (Canadian in the RAF, PoW 27.08.41), S/L R.A. Lee-Knight (RAF - OC), F/L B.S. Christmas, P/O P.R.M. Carrillo (American from New York City), P/O D.G.E. Ball (†22.03.43 as OC 411 Sqn), F/O L.E. Price (†21.01.44 in Canada while instructing), P/O L.S. Ford (†04.06.43, wing leader Digby Wing), F/O S.J. Reason (Eng.)
Front row:
Sgt C. Grigg, Sgt L.C. Sones (RAF), Sgt J.B.B Rainville, Sgt F.H. Belcher (PoW 06.04.42), F/O C. A. Hyde (RAF - Admin), Sgt E.A. Crist, Sgt K.V Collinson, Sgt G.A.J. Ryckman (†20.04.42, 402 Sqn), Sgt D.W. Cranham.

were seen. Pilot Officer C.J.P. Wood (RAF) was acting the Hornchurch wing leader's (W/C F.S. Stapleton) number two when they were engaged in fierce combat. Stapleton was flying a Spitfire Mk.VA while Wood was flying a Mk.II (P8090/H). They were on their way back when a squadron of Bf109s was reported at 11 o'clock at the same height (20,000 feet) 403 was flying at. They passed behind and Stapleton gave the order to keep a good look out in that direction. Indeed, the Germans soon attacked, two of them engaging the squadron. Stapleton pulled to the right and then went into a steep dive to the left. Wood followed his leader, but, in the dive, three Bf109s flying in loose formation from left to right, appeared. One fell immediately to Stapleton's fire while Wood singled one out on the right side of the formation. He opened fire from astern and above from about 200 yards, firing until only about 25 yards away. Wood saw smoke pouring from the engine, but then he had to pull up steeply to avoid colliding with the Bf109 which was seen spinning down. On the debit side, F/L E.C. Cathels a Canadian serving in the RAF and one of the two flight commanders, did not return and was captured, while P/O N.D.R. Dick (RCAF) collided with a Hurricane over the Channel, but managed to get back and make a forced landing at Manston. This would be the only major operation of the month and while 403 flew further sorties over the continent during that period of time, they were uneventful.

The days of the Spitfire II were numbered as, on 12 September, 403 received notice it would finally be converted back to the Spitfire V in a few days. In the meantime, the squadron continued to soldier on with the Spitfire II and, for its swansong, they participated in *Circus* 95 on the 17th. Operational activity had been limited since the beginning of the month with no incursions over the continent. The Luftwaffe was engaged, but no claims or losses were reported. In the afternoon the squadron was airborne again to patrol over ASR vessels searching for a downed pilot. Squadron Leader R.A. Lee-Knight and P/O C.J.P. Wood (RAF) observed enemy aircraft diving to attack the boats. Orders were given to attack and a combat took place 5-6 miles off Cap Gris Nez, the altitude varying from 1000 to 50 feet. The CO sealed the fate of one of the Bf109s, seen to descend in flames, while Wood got one as well, seen diving into the sea, plus another claimed as probably destroyed (seen with black and white smoke pouring from the engine). No loss was reported for the Canadians. That was the last op flown by the squadron's Mk.IIs as, over the next few days, the pilots carried out practice flights with Mk.Vs before returning to operations with their new mounts on the 20th. The connection between 403 Squadron and the Spitfire II was over, the mark leaving the unit after just 100 sorties.

Claims - 403 (RCAF) Squadron (Confirmed and Probable)

Date	*Pilot*	*SN*	*Origin*	*Type*	*Serial*	*Code*	*Nb*	*Cat.*
27.08.41	P/O Cyril P.J. **Wood**	RAF No. 69442	RAF	Bf109	**P8090**	KH-H	1.0	C
17.09.41	S/L Roland A. **Lee-Knight**	RAF No. 37772	RAF	Bf109	**P7445**	KH-L	1.0	C
	P/O Cyril P.J. **Wood**	RAF No. 69442	RAF	Bf109	**P7368**	KH-J	1.0	C
				Bf109			1.0	P

Total: 4.0

Summary of the aircraft lost on Operations - 403 (RCAF) Squadron

Date	*Pilot*	*S/N*	*Origin*	*Serial*	*Code*	*Fate*
27.08.41	F/L Edmund C. **Cathels**	RAF No. 37905	(CAN)/RAF	**P8726**	KH-G	**PoW**

Total: 1

Summary of the aircraft lost by accident - 403 (RCAF) Squadron

Date	*Pilot*	*S/N*	*Origin*	*Serial*	*Code*	*Fate*
30.07.41	Sgt Lesa **Girman**	Can./ R.71250	RCAF	**P7825**	KH-C	†

Total: 1

No. 411 (RCAF) Squadron (code DB)

As the fourth fighter squadron of the RCAF overseas, 411 was formed at Digby on 16 June 1941. Command was given to F/L P.B. Pitcher (RCAF) who was posted in from 401 Squadron where he had been serving as a flight commander. Over the next few days, 411 received its complement of eighteen Spitfire Mk.Is while the two flight commanders arrived at the squadron. Flying Officers K.A. Boomer and R.C. Weston both RCAF were promoted to flight lieutenant upon arrival as more pilots continued to join the new unit. Training commenced with the old Spitfires, but these were soon replaced by Mk.IIs, the first two, P7827/H and P8276, taken on charge from 616 Squadron on 17 July. The replacement process was accelerated with the arrival of P7595/G, P7755, P7679/F, P7880/Q, P7915/B, P7923/R, P7926/N, P7964, P8076, P8172/A, P8263/C and P8371 by the end of the month. P7964 had a short stay as, during take off on 23 July, P/O E.C. Cryderman (RCAF) raised the undercarriage too early causing the aircraft to settle back on the ground. It was sent to a MU for repairs. Worse was to come, sadly, when, one week later on the 29th, Sgt R.M. Murray, an American serving in the RCAF became separated from his leader owing to poor visibility during formation practice and was seen soon after at low altitude before eventually crashing at Pyewipe Mudflats, Great Coates. The aircraft was embedded deep in the mud and few remains were recovered. More new Spitfires were taken on in August to make up for attrition and to raise the squadron to its full strength (P7603/Z, P8136/S, P8657/V and P8663/X). Even though the squadron was not fully operational (this would be achieved on 27 August), two Spitfire Mk.IIs were scrambled on the 21st, opening 411's operational log. The two pilots were P/O

D.J.M. Blakeslee, another American serving in the RCAF, and Sgt J.W. Sills (RCAF). Incidentally, further scrambles were flown before the squadron became fully operational, but all proved uneventful. From the 27th onwards, 411 was allowed to fly offensive ops, but the days were spent performing convoy patrols instead.

In the first few days of September, 411 was preparing to fly its first offensive operation, but it was cancelled each time for one reason or another, the process generating some frustration. Up to 20 September only a few operational sorties were flown (mainly patrols or scrambles). The first participation in a 'show' took place on the 20th with the Canadian 401 and the Rhodesian 266. The Wing was led by a Canadian serving in the RAF, W/C H.P. Blatchford, and the op was executed without incident. The next day another sweep was carried out with the same results, 412 replacing 401 on this occasion. The next sweep was flown on the 27th with the same trio as the 21st. So far, while Bf109s had been seen, they had not been engaged. On this occasion, however, they were. Individual dogfights ensued over the French coast near Mardyck. Flight Lieutenant K.A. Boomer was seen to be pursued by Bf109s, but he shook them off in an evasive turn and managed to fire a burst at one of them and claim it as damaged. Flying Officer R.W. McNair did the same using his machine guns only. In the meantime, the Spitfire flown by Sgt J.D. McFarlane (American) was hit by flak, but he managed to glide to within a few hundred yards of the English coast before he baled out at 2000 feet. He drifted a few yards beyond the cliffs at Beachy Head with a few small pieces of shrapnel in one leg for his effort. This raid involved the last operational sorties carried out before the end of the month. Operational activity remained low in early October. The squadron was not inactive, far from it, as it had started the transition to the Spitfire Mk.V and was fully occupied with acceptance test flights. Despite this, and even though some patrols were already being flown by the new mark, 411 participated in a major sweep on 13 October with a mixed fleet of Spitfires, the bulk being Mk.IIs. The squadron was again flying with 412 and 266 Squadrons. Things were going well up until the formation turned for home. On the return journey, a few miles from Boulogne, F/O R.W. McNair (RCAF) found himself on his own. Shortly after, he heard over the R/T there were scattered groups of Bf109s off Boulogne. He flew in that direction at about 28,000 feet and observed a number of aircraft below at quite a low altitude. He dived to about 5000 feet then pulled up over the sea before entering a shallower dive. He saw enemy aircraft circling a pilot in the water. He singled out one of the Bf109s and fired at it, but the Bf109 entered a sharp diving turn to the left to evade. McNair followed and delivered a second burst before pulling out. He then saw the Bf109 hit the sea, but did not see a parachute. McNair then headed for base, but in turn became the target of one of the Bf109s and was engaged in a furious dogfight. He managed to fire a burst to damage his assailant, but the Spitfire was soon badly hit and he was obliged to bale out at 400 feet. Fortunately, rescue arrived within fifteen minutes. The next day, Canadian Sergeants T.D. Holden and J.M. Reid scrambled in what would be the final operational sorties for the Spitfire Mk.II with 411 Squadron. The unit was fully operational on the Mk.V the next day. The Canadians had flown 133 sorties with the Mk.II.

Claims - 411 (RCAF) Squadron (Confirmed and Probable)

Date	Pilot	SN	Origin	Type	Serial	Code	Nb	Cat.
13.10.41	P/O Robert W. **McNair**	Can./ J.4745	RCAF	Bf109	**P7679**	DB-F	1.0	C

Total: 1.0

Spitfire II P7923/DB-R of 411 Sqn at Digby during the summer of 1941.

Date	Pilot	S/N	Origin	Serial	Code	Fate
27.09.41	Sgt John D. **McFarlane**	Can./ R.73033	(us)/RAF	**P8172**	DB-A	-
13.10.41	P/O Robert W. **McNair**	Can./ J.4745	RCAF	**P7679**	DB-F	-

Total: 2

'Buck' McNair who would become one of top aces of the RCAF made his first claims on Spitfire Mk II. A Canadian from Nova Scotia, he joined the RCAF in June 1940. After his training in Canada, he sailed for the UK in March 1941, attended No. 58 OTU, and was then posted to No. 411 (RCAF) Squadron in June. He opened his score on 27 September 1941 by damaging a Bf109. Two weeks later he added a confirmed Bf109 and another damaged, but was shot down and subsequently rescued. In February 1942 he volunteered to serve on Malta and, upon his arrival in March, was posted to No. 249 (Gold Coast) Squadron. In about two months he became one of the unit's most notable pilots, gaining many successes and claims (over fifteen) and by mid-June, when he left the island, he had also become a flight commander and a DFC recipient (the decoration received in May). He returned to the UK where he re-joined No. 411 (RCAF) Squadron and continued making claims until September when his tour expired and he was sent home. After taking part in war bonds publicity, he was briefly posted to No. 133 Squadron RCAF in Canada before sailing once more to the UK in March 1943 where he flew as supernumerary with Nos. 412 (RCAF) and 403 (RCAF) Squadrons before taking command of No. 416 (RCAF) Squadron in May and No. 421 (RCAF) Squadron the following month. With 421, McNair made his final claims, the last, a Fw190 destroyed, taking place on 3 October 1943. His score had then reached sixteen confirmed victories, five probables and fourteen damaged. During that period, he added a Bar to his DFC in July and a second Bar in October. He was shot down again on 20 July and suffered severe burns to his face. In mid-October he was promoted to Wing Commander and became the Wing Leader of No. 126 (RCAF) Wing. He led the wing until April 1944 as the effect of the flames on his face had begun to affect his vision. On leaving the wing he was made a Companion of the DSO. No further operational postings followed before the end of the war. He stayed in the post-war RCAF until his death through illness in January 1971.

Date	Pilot	S/N	Origin	Serial	Code	Fate
30.07.41	Sgt Robert M. **Murray**	Can./ R.68488	(us)/RCAF	**P7755**		†

Total: 1

No. 412 (RCAF) Squadron (code VZ)

Formed at Digby on 30 June 1941, 412 (RCAF) Squadron was equipped with Spitfires from the start. Command was given to S/L C.W. Trevena, a Battle of Britain veteran with 1 Squadron RCAF. The first two aircraft were taken on charge on the 7th as personnel joined daily. These two Spitfires were made serviceable by the evening of the 8th and the first four local flights were immediately flown. The following days included further flying while five more Spitfires arrived, the squadron flying a mixed force of Spitfire Mk.Is and IIs with the majority being the newer aircraft. The first days of practice were marred by two minor mishaps without major consequences for pilots and aircraft. Training intensified as more pilots and aircraft arrived. On 2 August, 412 suffered loss for the first time when Sergeants Smith and McLean collided in flight. Smith, flying Mk.I X4176 at the time, was killed. McLean managed to return home. Another death was sadly reported at the end of the month when P/O W.R. Hughes, flying a Spitfire II, collided in mid-air with a Hampden over Waddington at around 12.10. Nobody survived the collision. By the end of August, only Spitfire IIs remained on squadron charge: P7198, P7281, P7759, P7777/N, P7782, P7837, P7856/E, P7918, P8086/B, P8145/K, P8250/F, P8369/G, P8397, P8472/T and P8571/R. The previous day, the 30th, the squadron had been declared operational.

The first week was disappointing as no operations were carried out. A scramble was ordered on the 7th, but it proved to be uneventful. The squadron had to wait until the 12th to fly again on operations (convoy patrols), with more following over the next few days. The first offensive op was flown on the 21st, a Wing sweep over the north coast of France (Circus 101) in company with the Rhodesian 266 and the Canadian 411 (412 flying in the middle of the formation at 21,000 feet). While the enemy was sighted, he was not engaged. The squadron participated in another Wing sweep on the 27th (Circus 103), but though the Wing engaged the Luftwaffe, 412 had an uneventful time of it. In all, the squadron achieved a little more than 100 sorties in September. Excluding the two sweeps, convoy patrols made up the rest of the month's operational effort. Between late September and the beginning of October, 412 was involved in various Army-cooperation exercises at Boscombe Down. The pilots returned to Digby on 3 October, but bad weather prevented any operational flying and the pilots had to wait until the 10th before ops could be flown again. On the 8th the squadron received its first Spitfire Mk.Vs and these were put into service alongside the Mk.IIs. There was nothing much doing until the 13th when a Wing sweep was flown with 266 and 411 Squadrons. They headed to West Malling to carry out Circus 108A. They patrolled the north coast of France from Boulogne and south of Hardelot to cover the withdrawal of a RAF bomber formation. The squadron was flying at 25,000 feet in loose formation, in the middle of the Wing formation, with 266 flying below and 411 above. A number of Bf109s were sighted flying at 27,000 feet. Pilot Officer A.P.L. Smith saw one diving from the northeast to his left. He turned and fired at it, but didn't register any hits. In the afternoon, the squadron received orders to return base at 13.45 and Sgt E.N. Macdonell found himself separated from the squadron. Seeing some Spitfires below at 10,000 feet, he decided to join them when he observed two Bf109s flying line astern. He dived and attacked out of the sun, opening fire at 12,000 feet with a five second burst at the rear Bf109. MacDonnell saw bullets strike the cockpit and the Bf109 immediately went into a dive. Following closely, Macdonell fired several short bursts at intervals. The enemy aircraft made no other attempt at evasive action and MacDonnell started to pull out, when he was doing 400 mph, and blacked out. When he recovered his vision he found himself 400 feet over the water and, after circling, he saw no sign of the enemy aircraft so returned to West Malling. Wing Commander P.G. Jameson, the wing leader, who was passing by, noticed shortly afterwards a large patch of oil on the water so the claim was credited as a confirmed kill, the first for 412. This was to be the last major operation for the Spitfire II as more Mk.Vs arrived. The Mk.IIs were withdrawn, but continued to fly some convoy patrols. The last sorties were recorded on the 20th for a total of 162. From that point 412 Squadron was fully operational unit on the Spitfire V.

Date	Pilot	SN	Origin	Type	Serial	Code	Nb	Cat.
13.10.41	Sgt Edward N. **Macdonell**	Can./ R.60241	RCAF	Bf109	**P7856**	VZ-E	1.0	C

Total: **1.0**

Date	Pilot	S/N	Origin	Serial	Code	Fate
31.08.41	P/O William R. **Hugues**	Can./ J.5483	RCAF	**P8586**		†

Total: **1**

Paul Webb joined the Auxiliary Air Force in 1937 with 602 Sqn and was called up for active service in September 1939. He participated in the Battle of Britain, but was wounded in combat on 16 August and did not return to operational duties until the following year when he became a flight commander with 123 Sqn in May 1941. He assumed command of 416 Sqn in November 1941. In March 1942 he left for the Middle East and Malta and in May 1944 took over 253 Sqn before becoming wing leader of 281 Wing. Webb remained in the RAF after the war on a Permanent Commission and retired in 1973 as an Air Commodore.

No. 416 (RCAF) Squadron (code DN)

The RCAF overseas continued to expand and 416 Squadron was formed on 22 November 1941 at Peterhead, near Aberdeen, in Scotland. It was the sixth fighter RCAF squadron to be formed overseas. Command was given to the newly promoted S/L P.C. Webb, previously a flight commander with 123 Squadron. A British pilot, he served with 602 Squadron during the Battle of Britain. He was tasked with getting the new unit up to operational standard. It was intended from the start the Spitfire Mk.II would be used as the squadron was not on the frontline. The first aircraft arrived by air on 25 November (P8397 and P8472). Three days later, P7897, P8145, P8369 and P8391 were added to the inventory. The squadron was reeling on 30 November when F/L K.C. Jackman, the first flight commander recently posted in, was killed when the airfield was strafed in the morning by a German raider. In the process, one Spitfire was also damaged and had to be sent away for repairs.

During the first days of December, 416 saw its two flight commanders posted in, C.F. Bradley from 132 Squadron and J.D. Keynes, both British while, during the month, more Spitfires were taken on charge (P7553, P7698, P7856, P7918/S, P7920, P7982, P7989, P8162, P8275/P, P8379 and P8598). The first prang was recorded on the 19th when Sgt R.A. Buckham (RCAF) ran off the runway and nosed over, fortunately with nothing more than a slightly damaged propeller. At the end of January, 416 received a cannon-armed Spitfire IIB (possibly P8650) to allow the pilots to familiarise themselves with the weapon they would soon use when the Mk.Vs finally arrived. On 30 January, 416 was put on readiness as a nearby town was attacked by a Ju88, but bad weather prevented any take off. At that time, the squadron could count on 32 pilots in its ranks.

More activity was noted in February with the first operational sorties. On 1 February, P/O P.G. Blades (RCAF) scrambled, but an interception could not be made. During the month, 416 was involved in various scrambles or patrols, all uneventful or a friendly aircraft the culprit, representing about forty sorties. On the debit side, F/L Keynes wrecked a Spitfire on the 6th while trying to take off from an icy runway. The Spitfire skidded into a snow bank and was still there the next day when a Stirling (W6086) crashed into it and totally demolished the Spitfire. In the middle of the month, 416 was notified the three RAF leaders were to be posted out and replaced with RCAF ones (effective on the 18th for the two flight commanders). This left the squadron without any commanders for a couple of days. By the end of the month F/L L.V. Chadburn had taken over A Flight while B Flight's command was assumed by F/L W.W. Murray. Chadburn eventually took over the squadron on 9 March, finally replacing P.C. Webb who was posted overseas. A Flight was handed over to F/L P.L. Archer's guiding hand. About that time, the first Spitfire Mk.Vs appeared on strength and both marks flew side by side for a short time. When 416 moved to Dyce, in Scotland, on 14 March, it was only equipped with the Spitfire V, marking the end of the Spitfire II on ops. The squadron flew just 76 sorties, 37 of them in March, with the Mk.II.

Summary of the aircraft lost by accident - 416 (RCAF) Squadron

Date	Pilot	S/N	Origin	Serial	Code	Fate
07.02.42	*Ground accident*	-	-	**P7982**	DN-M	-
				Total: 1		

William Pentland from Alberta was posted from 402 Squadron in December 1941 to take over B Flight. He would complete his first tour of operations in June 1943 with 417. For his second tour of operation, he would lead 440 in Europe flying Typhoons until being killed in action on 7 October. He had been awarded the DFC in September.

No. 417 (RCAF) Squadron (code AN)

This unit was formed on 27 November 1941 at Charmy Down. The formation was quick as, by 1 December, the squadron already had 22 pilots in its ranks, sixteen of them NCOs. However, most were recent graduates from OTUs. Command was assumed by S/L C.E. Malfroy, a New Zealander serving in the RAF and a Battle of France and Britain veteran. That day, the first Spitfire Mk.IIs arrived, most passed on by 313 (Czech) Squadron: P7544, P7602, P7834, P8071, P8192 and P8667. They were soon followed by P7310, P7320, P7353, P7687, P7983, P8018, P8132, P8168, P8186, P8201 and P8508. It was not planned to use the type on operations, but they would enable the squadron to work up to operational status. Training began slowly, however, and it was not until the middle of the month that 417 achieved an effective flying tempo. More than 180 hours were logged by the end of the month.

Training continued in January 1942 and, excluding three minor accidents, the month was uneventful. However one of the minor accident led to the write-off of P7544 while parked when Sgt D.C. Goudie (RCAF) taxying into it struck it and damaged it so badly that it was later declared unrepairable and struck off charge the following 4 April. Some turnover of aircraft occurred as about a third of the fleet was due for inspection. Regarding ground personnel, 417 reached its operational requirements at the beginning of February. Soon after, on 6 February, F/L W.H. Pentland (RCAF), the B Flight CO, flew to Digby with five pilots to collect Spitfire Mk.Vs, thus signalling the phasing out of the Mk.II with the squadron. In all, 27 Spitfire Mk.IIs were employed by 417. This was a high number for such a short time period, but it can be explained by various minor accidents, six all up, and also because some aircraft were war weary and needed inspection or major overhaul (as was the case for four of them).

Summary of the aircraft lost by accident - 417 (RCAF) Squadron

Date	Pilot	S/N	Origin	Serial	Code	Fate
06.01.42	*Ground accident*	-	-	**P7544**		-
				Total: 1		

No. 485 (NZ) Squadron (code OU)

New Zealand, via the Empire Air Training Scheme, raised its first squadron, 485, on 1 March 1941 at Driffield in Yorkshire. Chosen to lead the squadron was S/L M.C.B. Knight, a New Zealander serving in the RAF since 1935. The two flight commanders were also Kiwis enlisted in the RAF: Flight Lieutenants F.N. Brinsden and J.C. Martin. All were Battle of Britain veterans. The squadron worked up on Spitfire Mk.Is and was declared operational in mid-April. The old Spitfires were soon replaced by Mk.IIs in early June 1941. As there was no real difference between the marks, the pilots easily converted within a day and continued operational duties with barely an interruption. The first fifteen had arrived by 15 June. On 2 June, 485 carried out eighteen sorties across several convoy patrols. The change of mount brought luck for the Kiwis. Flight Lieutenant Brinsden and P/O R. Barrett were ordered to protect a convoy of thirty ships 12-15 miles off Hornsea late in the afternoon. After an hour, when flying below cloud, the section sighted an enemy aircraft (later identified as a Ju88) emerge from cloud and about 400 feet above. The Junkers probably saw the two New Zealanders as it immediately dropped its bombs some distance from the nearest ship and took violent evasive action, turning and climbing into cloud cover. Brinsden attacked and fired a burst, with full deflection, from about 250 yards, and followed it up with another short, but ineffective, burst from astern. Return fire from the Junkers was experienced and Brinsden received two bullets in the glycol header tank and oil cooler. Pilot Officer Barrett followed his leader in the attack and fired two short bursts. While he also experienced return fire, he was not hit, but could not claim to have damaged the German bomber. The Ju88 managed to disappear into cloud and contact was lost. The pair was replaced by F/L Martin and Sgt W.H. Russell who also encountered a Ju88, but the situation was less favourable and only Martin managed to fire two ineffective bursts. Another pair, Pilot Officers G.H. Francis and H.H. Thomas, arrived to continue to cover the convoy. They were patrolling at 1500 feet when they saw a Ju88 emerge from cloud about 500 feet above and on their left. The German crew saw the Spitfires as well and immediately turned to the left

485 Squadron founding members, Driffield, Spring 1941.
Rear, left to right: Corporal French (groundcrew), Sgt D.S. McGregor (†09.05.44 - 598 Sqn), P/O R. Barrett (†07.05.44 - 65 Sqn), P/O W.A. Middleton (†27.08.41), P/O G.H. Francis, P/O A.G. Shaw (a New Zealander in the RAF), F/L J.C. Martin (†27.08.41 - 222 Sqn, New Zealander in the RAF), S/L M.W.B. Knight, F/L F.N. Brinsden, P/O P.S. McBride, P/O A.G. McIntyre, Corporal T.G. Smith (groundcrew), LAC Bongard (groundcrew), LAC Erridge (groundcrew), Corporal Murray (groundcrew), LAC MacGibbon (groundcrew).
Front, left to right: Sgt George (groundcrew), LAC Neville (groundcrew), LAC Martin (groundcrew), Sgt H.L. Thomas, Sgt R.J. Bullen (†23.06.41), Sgt W.V. Crawford-Compton, Sgt J. Maney (†24.07.41), Sgt J.K. Porteous, Sgt A.B. Smith, Sgt H.N. Sweetman, Sgt K.D. Cox (†18.06.41).
(Paul Sortehaug)

and climbed for cloud. It was followed by Francis who fired a short burst from 300 yards before closing in with a two second burst. Sergeant Thomas followed, firing a long burst, and strikes were seen along the fuselage. Some of his bullets struck aft the cockpit and pieces were seen flying off. That was all they could do as the Ju88 found safety in the cloud and contact was lost. It was claimed as damaged, however, to open 485's score. Later, the final pair, the CO and P/O A.G. McIntyre, the latter being a New Zelander serving in the RAF began their patrol. At about 22.25, as darkness set in, a Ju88 was sighted below cloud about one mile to the right. Squadron Leader Knight immediately attacked and observed strikes along the left side of the fuselage as well as the wing roots and engine. Return fire was experienced, but was silenced at once. The Junkers entered cloud with its left engine on fire and smoke issuing from the right engine. Nothing else could be done, but later on the naval escort reported a Ju88 had crashed into the sea. It was the squadron's first confirmed kill of the war. Operational activity continued during the month, but no further encounters occurred. However, 485 lost two pilots in June. Sergeant K.D. Cox was killed doing aerobatics on the 18th. His Spitfire was seen to crash from 800 feet as he was performing a slow roll. The second loss occurred a few days later on the 23rd when Sgt R.J. Bullen was posted missing. That day 485 carried its first Wing patrol over the French coast. Bullen became separated from the other three in his section and reported he was continuing the patrol alone. While returning from the French coast at 7000 feet, he was found being attacked by Bf109s from astern. Hit, the Spitfire ended up on its back as it spun towards the sea with clouds of white and black smoke coming from the engine. During the final week of June, the nature of the operational activity turned to the offensive and no less than four more Wing sweeps were flown, but all were uneventful. By the end of the month, the Spitfire Mk.IIs in service with the squadron were P7438/Q, P7566/Z, P7605/N, P7621/Y, P7697/B, P7758/F, P7773/D, P7785, P7788/E, P7821, P7822/A, P7916, P7964, P7974/L, P7908, P7961, P7975/R, P7977/U, P7986/G and P8025/P.

After completing just over 200 sorties in June, July would see close to 450 more flown during the month. This increase in activity was the consequence of the move from Leconsfield to Redhill at the beginning of the month. The move was also accompanied with a change of leadership as P/O E.P. Wells had succeeded F/L Martin as A Flight Leader a couple of days before. On 3 July 485 carried out two operations, one in the morning and one in the afternoon, but both proved uneventful. Another was flown the next day, along with some convoy patrols, but the enemy was not engaged. An engagement finally took place on the 5th during an escort for three Stirlings to Lille. The squadron took off shortly after midday and, while over Lille about one hour later, now F/L Wells saw a Bf109 make a very faint-hearted pass at the bombers and continue its dive at high speed, passing near Wells and his wingman, P/O R.H. Strang. Wells immediately moved into a good position and, allowing for full deflection, fired a quick burst before following the fleeing aircraft down. Wells fired one more short burst and then broke away out of the vertical dive. The German pilot was seen to bale out soon after. Proceeding home, and trying to catch up with the rest of the squadron in the distance, Wells noticed several Bf109s flying towards them immediately above. He called out a warning and at the same time turned slightly and saw two more Bf109s flying a bit below in wide abreast formation. He decided to close in on the nearest one and did so without much difficulty. Apparently unobserved, Wells was able to fire a two second burst from 250 yards and slightly to one side. The Bf109 started a climbing turn, which Wells was able to follow easily, before another two second burst blew off the hood and black smoke began pouring out. As the Bf109 was pulling up higher, Wells delivered a third two second burst from very close range. The German pulled up even steeper, stalled and started to spin. As he flicked over, Wells saw flames coming from the sides of the fuselage which was probably burning petrol pouring out of the stricken airframe. Wells was attacked at that moment so had to evade violently, but he eventually returned home to make a double claim. The New Zealanders sustained no loss. The 6th and 7th were also busy with escorts and patrols, as were the 8th and 9th, but during the Circus on the 8th Sgt W.H. Hendry was posted missing. He was last seen off Gravelines. That same afternoon, P/O C. Stewart, a New Zealander serving in the RAF redressed the balance when he sent a Bf109 into the Channel off Calais during a coastal cover patrol led by W/C J.R.A. Peel. Sadly, Stewart did not have the opportunity to score again as he was posted missing three days later after a fighter sweep in almost the same area. The squadron was attacked by six enemy fighters at 23,000 feet. Stewart was last seen over the Straits of Dover. The pressure was maintained with close to 200 sorties carried out between the 12th and the 23rd, but 485 would have to wait until the 24th to report success. That day, while escorting bombers to Cherbourg, F/L E.P. Wells destroyed a Bf109 near the town, his fifth confirmed victory (he had achieved his first two with 41 Squadron), but this was balanced by the loss of Sgt J. Maney. He was seen being shot down and descending safely under his parachute about 15 miles north of Cherbourg. Despite this, he and his aircraft were lost without trace. The last week of July was less intense and 485 only performed patrols during which nothing of importance happened. A new B Flight leader, F/L S.C. Norris, assumed his role from the 22nd. This low rate of operations continued during early August with just some Rhubarbs flown. It was not until the 5th that the squadron returned over the continent on a Circus that could not be completed because of bad weather. The next day, 485 performed a cover patrol off Dungeness without incident. On the 7th, 485 participated in Circus 67 during which Sgt C.S.V. Goodwin failed to return. He was later reported as a PoW. That day, the Wing was engaged over Saint-Omer and Goodwin was shot down by Fw190s, baling out of his flaming Spitfire. He was captured with burns to his wrists and face, very common injuries as these areas were often the pilot's only exposed skin, and spent some time in hospital before being transferred to a PoW

Among the Kiwi pilots who made claims while flying the Spitfire II, two would become outstanding pilots.

Left, 'Hawkeye' Wells. He was one of the key leaders, as a flight commander, of 485 Sqn during the late summer and autumn of 1941 and was one of the regular scorers during that period. Before joining 485, he served with 41 Sqn during the Battle of Britain where he made his initial claims. Later on, Wells was given command of 485 before being promoted to lead the Kenley Wing. He ended the war with a DSO, DFC and Bar. After the war he served with the RNZAF and then the RAF before retiring June 1960. *(via P. Sortehaug)* Right, Jack Rae did not remain in the UK and was posted to Malta, where he joined 603 Sqn, and later played an active part in the Siege of Malta with 249 Sqn. Returning to the UK with a DFC, he re-joined 485 Sqn for a second tour of operations, but was shot down and made a PoW on 22.08.43. *(J.D. Rae)*

camp. The squadron seemed to be running out of luck. While the two following fighter sweeps over the continent were eventful, the Circus that followed on the 12th saw two more pilots lost. Sergeant G.M. Porter, a New Zealander serving in the RAF was killed and Sgt W.H. Russell joined Goodwin at the hospital in Saint-Omer. He was so severely injured he had to have an arm amputated and was eventually repatriated in 1943. Two days later, the squadron began to re-equip with Spitfire Mk.Vs, but would continue to fly the Mk.II for a little while longer. On 16 August a mixed force, led by S/L Knight, flew an offensive sweep first thing in the morning and, around midday, acted as support cover to Circus 74. In the course of this operation various engagements developed and Sgt L.J. Frecklington, flying a Mk.II, claimed a Bf109 probably destroyed near Cap Gris Nez while Sgt L.P. Griffiths, who was also flying a Mk.II, claimed another as damaged. A third claim was made by F/L Wells, but he was flying a Mk.V. The re-equipment continued rapidly over the next few days and the last Spitfire II sorties were carried out on the morning of the 19th during Circus 82. An engagement took place on the return journey before the squadron reached the French coast. Sergeant J.D. Rae saw a 485 Spitfire (Sgt K.C.M. Miller) being attacked and mortally hit. It was last seen diving with glycol streaming behind. He then saw the Bf109 begin to manoeuver to repeat his attack on Rae. A violent dogfight ensued at the end of which Rae was able to fire a two second burst. The Bf109 spun into the ground out of control. This was revenge for Miller who was reported as killed in action. An evening Lysander escort was performed entirely with Spitfire Mk.Vs (see *SQUADRONS!* 31), so Rae's victory proved a fitting end for the squadron's time with the Mk.II. In all, 485 flew about 800 sorties on their old mounts.

Claims - 485 (NZ) Squadron (Confirmed and Probable)

Date	Pilot	SN	Origin	Type	Serial	Code	Nb	Cat.
02.06.41	S/L Marcus W.B. **KNIGHT**	RAF No. 37408	(NZ)/RAF	Bf109	**P7773**	OU-D	1.0	C
05.07.41	F/L Edward P. **WELLS**	NZ39950	RNZAF	Bf109	**P8022**	OU-Y	2.0	C
08.07.41	P/O Charles **STEWART**	RAF No. 44231	(NZ)/RAF	Bf109	**P7822**	OU-A	1.0	C
24.07.41	F/L Edward P. **WELLS**	NZ39950	RNZAF	Bf109	**P8022**	OU-Y	1.0	C
16.08.41	Sgt Lindsay J. **FRECKLINGTON**	NZ401261	RNZAF	Bf109	**P7438**	OU-Q	1.0	P
19.08.41	Sgt John D. **RAE**	NZ402896	RNZAF	Bf109	**P7621**	OU-Y	1.0	C

Total: 7.0

Date	Pilot	S/N	Origin	Serial	Code	Fate
23.06.41	Sgt Richard J. **Bullen**	NZ40753	RNZAF	**P7975**	OU-R	†
08.07.41	Sgt William N. **Hendry**	NZ39067	RNZAF	**P8470**	OU-S	†
11.07.41	P/O Charles **Stewart**	RAF No. 44231	(NZ)/RAF	**P7773**	OU-D	†
24.07.41	Sgt Jack **Maney**	NZ40240	RNZAF	**P7831**	OU-G	†
07.08.41	Sgt Charles S.V. **Goodwin**	NZ401758	RNZAF	**P7594**	OU-G	**PoW**
12.08.41	Sgt George M. **Porter**	RAF No. 931283	(NZ)/RAF	**P7788**	OU-E	†
	Sgt William H. **Russell***	NZ40987	RNZAF	**P7970**	OU-D	**PoW**
19.08.41	Sgt Keith C.M. **Miller**	NZ401761	RNZAF	**P7977**	OU-U	†

Total: 8

* Severely wounded and repatriated in October 1943

Some other 485's casualties during the summer 1941. Photo on the left, Sgt Jack Maney, first from left on who was killed on 24 July 1941 and Sgt 'Vic' Goodwin third from left who became a PoW two weeks after Jack Maney was killed. In the middle , Sgt 'Hal' Thomas
(V.P. Goodwin)
Photo on the right, Sgt K.C.M. Miller, the last 485's casualty on Spitfire II.
(Miller family)

Summary of the aircraft lost by accident - 485 (NZ) Squadron

Date	Pilot	S/N	Origin	Serial	Code	Fate
18.06.41	Sgt Kevin D. **Cox**	NZ401257	RNZAF	**P7858**	OU-F	†

Total: 1

THE EAGLE SQUADRONS

No. 71 (Eagle) Squadron (code XR)

Re-formed in October 1940, this unit was the first of the three fighter squadrons to be raised with American volunteers. While the pilots were mostly American, the groundcrew were British. The squadron became operational with Hurricanes and, by the summer of 1941, like many other Fighter Command squadrons, had begun its transition to the Spitfire. At that time, 71 was based at North Weald. The first Spitfire Mk.IIs were taken on charge between 6 and 12 August 1941 (P7430, P7610, P7738, P7776, P7818, P7987, P8033/T, P8080, P8169, P8375, P8396, P8423/S, P8436 and P8702). The squadron was commanded by a British pilot, S/L H. de C.A. Woodhouse, but he was soon replaced by another British officer, S/L E.R. Bitmead, who, in turn, led for just a week before having to relinquish command due to poor health. He was replaced by S/L S.T. Meares from the 22nd. While the COs were British, the flight commanders were Americans: F/L A.B. Mamedoff from Connecticut (A Flight) and F/L C.G. Peterson from Idaho (B Flight). Conversion was quick, but it came at a cost with the death of P/O K.S. Taylor on the 8th during a practice flight. He hit the ground while recovering from a dive and was killed instantly. Taylor was born in Canada, but at least one of his parents was American. The first operational sorties, some convoy patrols, were flown on the 17th. Even the Hurricanes continued to fly operationally for the next two days. On the evening of the 20th, 71 participated in the first sweep with its first aircraft (led by F/L Mamedoff). That was followed the next day by two bomber escorts, one in the morning and one in the afternoon, both led by Mamedoff. All were uneventful if we exclude some aircraft returning early due to engine trouble. After a couple of days of reduced operational activity, 71 returned over the continent on the 25th with the new CO in the lead, but returned with nothing to report. That day, the first Rhubarbs were also flown. On the 27th, 71 participated in Circus 86, an escort for nine Blenheims to Lille. On the return journey, the squadron was flying at 17,000 feet when P/O W.R. Dunn developed oxygen trouble. He had to descend to 8000 feet as a result and flew below the bombers. At about five miles from the French coast a Bf109 attacked him from above and behind, but slightly overshot Dunn in the dive. Dunn raised the nose of his Spitfire and gave him a three second burst from 100 yards. Black and white smoke poured from the engine and the pilot baled out at about 7000 feet. Immediately after, another Bf109 made a similar attack, but it turned to the right to disengage. Dunn followed, managed to get in a good position, and gave a 4.5 second burst from 200 to 50 yards. The Bf109 burst into flames and crashed. This was not the end of the combat, however, as a third Bf109 appeared and was more accurate than its predecessors as its cannon fire struck Dunn's aircraft behind the cockpit rendering the R/T unserviceable and wounding his right foot in the process. The Bf109 continued its pursuit, but could not hit the Spitfire again. It eventually veered off and left the area. Dunn returned to base where he landed his damaged aircraft safely. He was off duty for a couple of weeks. Dunn's achievement was the first double claim made by a 71 Squadron pilot and would be the only ones made while flying the Spitfire Mk.II despite the rest of the month remaining busy. The squadron flew every day, carrying out eighty sorties during convoy patrols, Rhubarbs and bomber (29th) and destroyer escorts (31st). In the final days of August, the first Spitfire Mk.V arrived at the squadron. Indeed, 71 introduced the Mk.V on 1 September, but flew both types until mid-month. Two major operations, Circus ops, on the 1st and the 4th took care of the final combat work for the Spitfire IIs. After that date, the squadron flew the Mk.V. In all, 71 flew less than 250 sorties with the Spitfire Mk.II. (see *SQUADRONS!* 25)

William 'Wild Bill' Dunn from Minnesota was the first official American ace of WW2, but he was severely wounded the day he claimed his fourth and fifth victories. He later transferred to the USAAF in June 1943 and added to his score while flying P-47 Thunderbolts.

The Spitfire Mk.II, P7308/XR-D, in which William R. Dunn claimed two victories - the sole occasion a Mk.II of 71 Sqn was flown with success. Damage to the tail is clearly visible and Dunn was wounded during the combat, which resulted in him being repatriated.

Claims - 71 (Eagle) Squadron (Confirmed and Probable)

Date	Pilot	SN	Origin	Type	Serial	Code	Nb	Cat.
27.08.41	P/O William R. **Dunn**	RAF No. 60510	(us)/RAF	Bf109	**P7308**	XR-D	2.0	C

Total: 2.0

Summary of the aircraft lost by accident - 71 (Eagle) Squadron

Date	Pilot	S/N	Origin	Serial	Code	Fate
08.08.41	P/O Kenneth S. **Taylor**	RAF No. 64869	(us)/RAF	**P8572**		†

Total: 1

I was flying as Blue III with +No. 71 (Eagle) Squadron who were part of the escort wing to 9 Blenheims in Circus 86 on 27/8/41. We were flying at 17000 feet on the way back from Lille when I developed oxygen trouble. Because of this, I came down to 8000 feet and flew below the bombers. When about 5 miles away from the French coast a Me109F attacked me from above and behind. He slightly overshot me in his dive. I raised my nose and gave him a burst of three seconds from 100 yards range. Black and white smoke poured from his engine and the pilot baled out at about 7000 feet. A second Me.109F made a similar attack, but he turned to the right. I gave him a 4½ second burst from 200 to 50 yards. His plane burst into flames and crashed to the ground. A third Me109F continued the attack and his cannon fire struck my aeroplane behind the cockpit. It rendered my R/t unserviceable and wounded me in the right foot. I had now reached the French coast and he sheered off before I could return his fire. I was able to land my plane, which was damaged Cat. 2, at Hawkinge and I was taken to the Royal Victoria Hospital at Folkestone to have the broken bones in my foot set. I claim two 109F's destroyed.

W. R. Dunn P/O

No. 71 (Eagle) Squadron,
Royal   Air   Force.

Peter Powell became the first OC of 121 Sqn. A regular RAF officer, he started the war as a flight commander with 111 Sqn flying Hurricanes. He made his first claim as early as January 1940 and more followed over Dunkirk and during the Battle of Britain until he was rested in early August. He received the DFC in May 1940. Promoted to Wing Commander in January 1942, he became the wing leader of the Hornchurch Wing until June when wounds sustained in action kept him away from flying for a while. He later served in Tunisia and was commanding 121 Typhoon Wing at the end of the war.

No. 121 (Eagle) Squadron (code AV)

This unit was the second of the 'Eagle' squadrons and was formed (or re-formed as first formed in WW1) on 14 May 1941. Working up on Hurricanes, it was stationed at Kirton in Lindsey, between Sheffield and Hull, and it became operational at the end of July under the leadership of S/L R.P.R. Powell, a British officer. The two flight commanders, Flight Lieutenants H.C. Kennard and R.C. Wilkinson, were also British. The squadron flew occasional east coast convoy patrols and scrambles before conversion to the Spitfire II was undertaken. The type was, from the start, seen as an interim measure before Spitfire Mk.Vs were received and the squadron was sent south. The switch over took place from 19 October. The first local flights were carried out on the 19th and training continued until the end of the month without incident. On 1 November, the pilots heard they were to receive their first Mk.Vs before the end of the month. Convoy patrols were flown that day with F/L Kennard leading the first pair. The squadron returned to its previous operational activities with the Hurricane while intense training continued. The first Spitfires were tested over the next few days. The Spitfire Mk.II began on ops, but this only lasted until 17 November when an uneventful scramble was flown by Mk.Vs (see *SQUADRONS!* 25). The Spitfire II lasted about a month with 121, but still managed to complete 57 sorties.

The Spitfire IIs known to have served with 121 are: P7372, P7566, P7595, P7603/Z, P7811, P7827, P7828, P7915, P7926, P7985/P, P8076/M, P8133/T, P8136/S, P8276 and P8657/W.

No. 133 (Eagle) Squadron (code MD)

As the third 'Eagle' unit, 133 was formed on Hurricanes at Coltishall at the end of July. It became operational two months later, flying east coast convoy patrols most of the time. Squadron Leader G.A. Brown, a British officer, was in command and was supported by his two flight commanders, F/L H.A.S. Johnstone (British) and F/L A.B. Mamedoff (American). Mamedoff was replaced by another American, F/L C.E. Bateman from Massachusetts, when he was killed in a flying accident in a Hurricane. One month later, on 28 October, the first six Spitfires arrived (P7563, P7627, P8074, P8196, P8249 and P8256) and were immediately tested. The first Spitfire sorties, flown by Bateman and P/O F. Scudday from Texas, took place on 8 November. The patrol was uneventful. At that time, the squadron was continuing to use the Hurricane and would do so until the middle of December. In November, the Spitfire progressively assumed more and more of the workload as additional aircraft were taken on charge and training continued. At the end of the month, a new CO, S/L E.H. Thomas, arrived. On 30 November, P/O R.A. Wolfe, an American from Arkansas, got lost in bad weather due to radio failure, ran out of fuel and baled out over the Irish Free State. Interned, he managed to escape towards the end of 1943 and transferred to the USAAF in November that year. That was the only major event of the year. Otherwise, the squadron passed the end of 1941 quietly until 31 December when it moved to Kirton in Lindsey to operate over the continent. Their Spitfire Mk.IIs were left behind for Spitfire Mk.VAs on arrival (see *SQUADRONS!* 25). In all, 133 flew 105 sorties on Spitfire Mk.IIs between 8 November and 24 December 1941.

Summary of the aircraft lost by accident - 133 (Eagle) Squadron

Date	Pilot	S/N	Origin	Serial	Code	Fate
30.11.41	P/O Roland L. **WOLFE**	RAF No. 102518	(US)/RAF	**P8074**		**Int.**
	Total: 1					

Supermarine Spitfire Mk.IIA P7308
No. 71 (Eagle) Squadron
Pilot Officer William R. DUNN (USA)
North Weald (UK), August 1941

Supermarine Spitfire Mk.IIA P8136
No. 121 (Eagle) Squadron
Kirton-in-Lindsey (UK), November 1941

Supermarine Spitfire Mk.IIA P7315
No. 266 (Rhodesia) Squadron
Squadron Leader Patrick G. JAMESON
Wittering (UK), September 1940

Supermarine Spitfire Mk.IIA P7289
No. 266 (Rhodesia) Squadron
Flight Lieutenant Dennis L. ARTMITAGE
Wittering (UK), September 1940

Supermarine Spitfire Mk.IIB P8505
No. 266 (Rhodesia) Squadron
Wittering (UK), September 1941

Supermarine Spitfire Mk.IIA P7923
No. 411 (RCAF) Squadron
Digby (UK), summer 1941

Supermarine Spitfire Mk.IIA P7786
No. 452 (RAAF) Squadron
Sgt Keith B. CHILSHOLM (RAAF)
Kenley (UK), July 1941

Supermarine Spitfire Mk.IIA P8175
No. 457 (RAAF) Squadron
Jurby (UK), autumn 1941

SQUADRONS! - The series

Donald James Matthew BLAKESLEE DFC

Supermarine Spitfire Mk.VB EN031
No. 133 (Eagle) Squadron
Flight Lieutenant D. J. M. Blakeslee
CAN./ J.4551
Gravesend (UK), August 1942

Charles Cuthbertson LEARMONTH DFC*

Douglas Boston Mk. III A28-9 (01-AL891)
No. 22 Squadron RAAF
Squadron Leader C. C. Learmonth
Aus. 583
Port Moresby (New Guinea), spring 1943

Hans Anton MAURENBRECHER

Curtiss P-40N-35-CU C3-560
No. 120 (NEI) Squadron
Major H. Maurenbrecher
Biak (New Guinea), 1945-1946

Roland Prosper BEAMONT DSO* DFC*

Hawker Tempest Mk V JN*751
No. 150 Wing
Wing Commander R. P. Beamont
RAF No. 41819
Bradwell Bay (UK), April 1944

Ronald Thomas SUSANS DSO DFC

North American P-51D-25-NT A68-724
No. 77 squadron, RAAF
Squadron Leader R. T. Susans
O4391
Bofu (Japan), 1947

James Henry LACEY DFM*

Supermarine Spitfire Mk.XIV RN135
No. 17 Squadron
Squadron Leader J. H. Lacey
RAF No. 142709
Seletar (Singapore), autumn 1945

Introducing's RAF In Combat and Bravo Bravo Aviation's collection of
highly-detailed and historically accurate, high-quality aviation prints.
For more information on available prints, please visit :

or

Prints in connection with the book:

PL-050: DL Armitage
PL-052: KB Chisholm
PL-056: WR Dunn
PL-190: RPR Powell
PL-279: PG Jameson
PL-343: PB Pitcher